AF316724

Brainbows

A First Reference Book for Very Young Minds

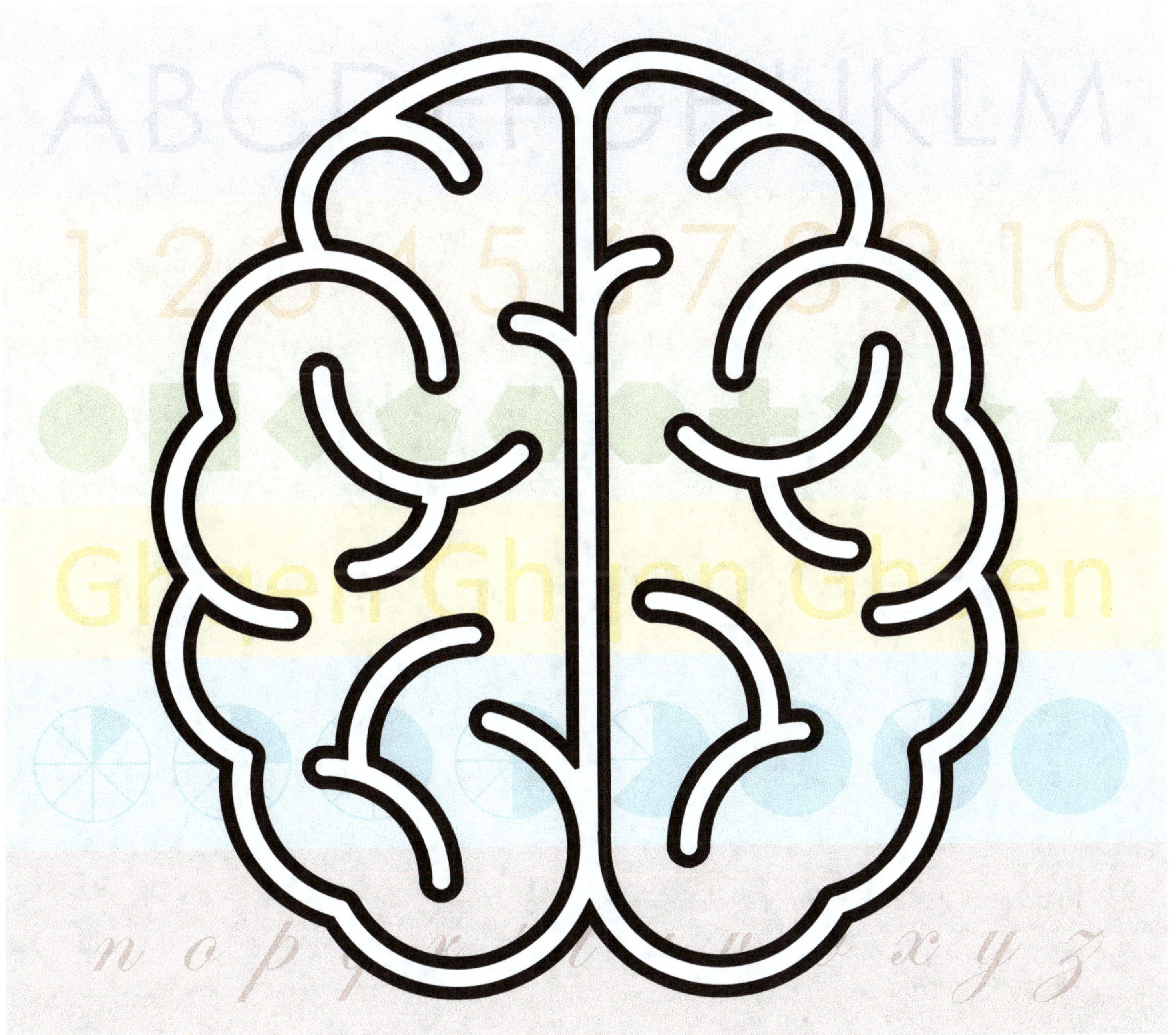

Jeff A. James

Version 1.12

To contact the author, email brainbowsbook@yahoo.com

ISBN 979-8-218-17599-3 Hardback
ISBN 978-1-0882-0271-5 Paperback

For Hannah,
Alice, and John

Foreword

I was a strange kid. As a small child, one of my favorite books was the dictionary. We had a big, thick, blue one. It was over 800 pages.

One of the things I loved about this dictionary was the general reference section at the end that included – among many other things – a listing of numbers. The listing started at one, then ten, then one hundred, one thousand, one million, and one billion. But the interesting part was that it kept going well after most such lists would stop. It included one trillion, then one quadrillion, then one quintillion, and so on all the way up to one duodecillion (which is a one followed by 39 zeroes). I remember using this information to educate my fourth grade teacher about some numbers that were beyond what she knew.

It occurred to me at some point that this dictionary was showing me an extension of knowledge that no other book had offered. I had many books as a child, but this one included something none of them had ever bothered to include. I also realized that the problem wasn't just limited to numbers.

Most color books for children included the basics: red, yellow, blue, green, purple, orange, black, and white. The really good books included a few extras such as brown, pink, or gray. Similarly, most shape books only included the same small handful: square, circle, triangle, rectangle, oval, and diamond. Occasionally you could find one with hexagon, heart, or semicircle.

I wanted more. What I really wanted was something more like my favorite dictionary, a reference book, one that included a more comprehensive list of colors, shapes, numbers, and other things I needed to know to round out my basic knowledge. But such a book didn't exist.

Many years later, I had children of my own, and I realized the state of books hadn't progressed much. We had a book of numbers that went all the way up to twenty, and a shape book that included some three-dimensional shapes such as cube and sphere. However, in general, the problem persisted. The book I wanted – a reference book for children – still didn't exist.

So I created it. This is that book.

As with any reference book, this book isn't intended to be read cover to cover. It's meant to be explored. It's meant to inspire questions and to be shared with others to understand the answers. It's meant for the young reader to discover something new each time they open its cover, with some pages becoming clear that perhaps didn't make sense a few months before.

Most of all, I hope your family enjoys it, and I hope everyone – from toddler to nonagenarian – is able to learn something new in its pages.

– Jeff A. James, December 2022

Colors

Colors

Colors

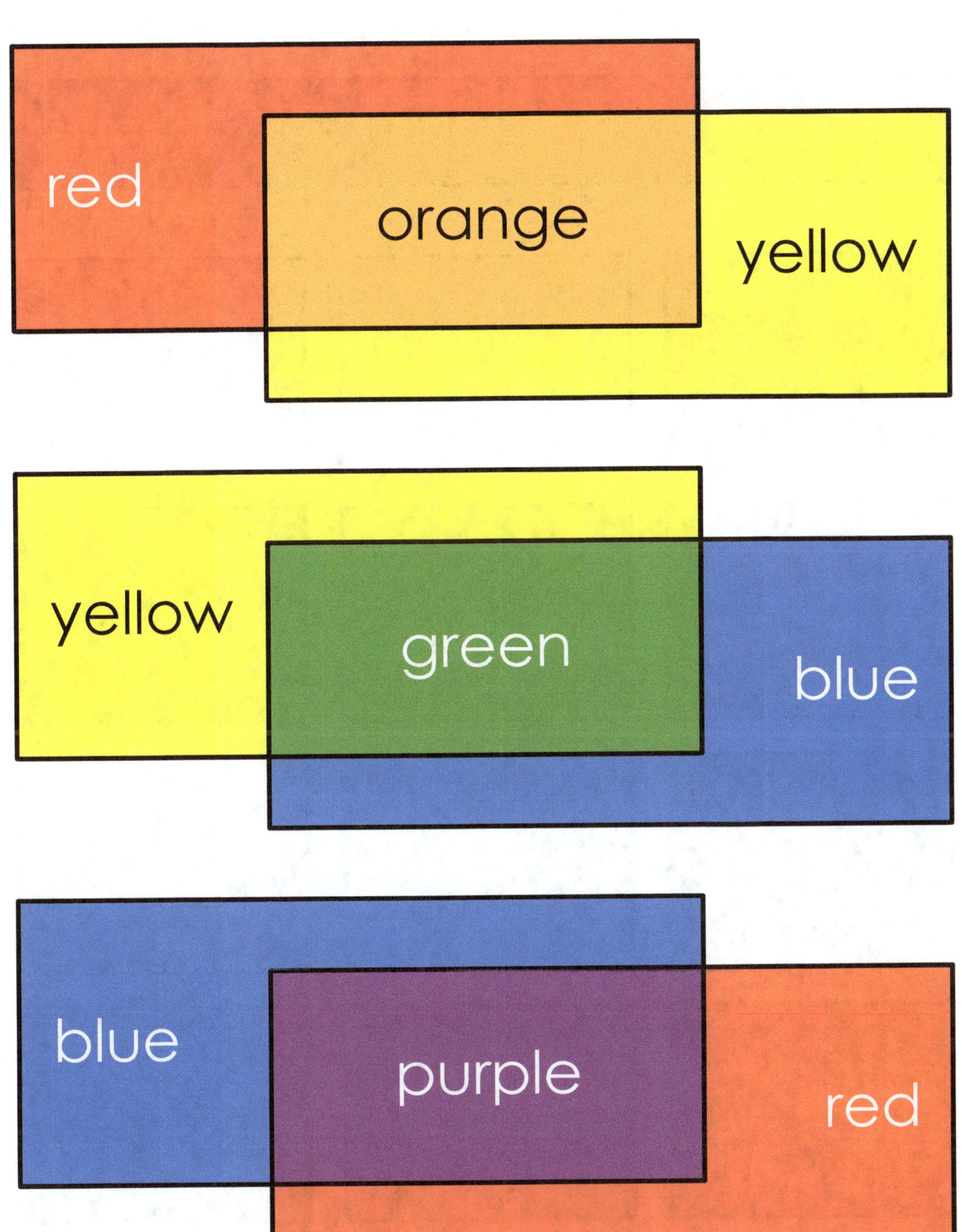

Colors

red

purple

crimson

pink

hot pink

amaranth

rose

magenta or fuchsia

maroon

puce

orchid

burgundy

eggplant

plum

Colors

purple blue

lavender	mauve	periwinkle
lilac	thistle	baby blue
amethyst	grape	sky blue
violet	indigo	deep violet

Colors

blue green

aqua or cyan	aquamarine	turquoise
ultramarine	verdigris	blue green
navy	teal	pine green
royal blue	cerulean	jade

Colors

green yellow

mint green	tea green	canary
chartreuse	green yellow	lime
emerald	lime green	kelly green
avocado	olive drab	olive

Colors

yellow orange

cream	blonde	peach
mustard	vanilla	buff
gold	saffron	topaz
amber	goldenrod	yellow orange

Colors

orange red

apricot	salmon	red orange
pumpkin	coral	scarlet
tangerine	tomato	vermilion
ochre	rust	auburn

Colors

brown
ivory
beige
copper
tan
bronze
chocolate
khaki
coffee
russet
ecru
taupe
sepia

Colors

white

light gray

gray

charcoal

black

Colors

Shapes, Symbols, and Patterns

Shapes, Symbols, and Patterns

Shapes

Shapes, Symbols, and Patterns

Shapes

Shapes, Symbols, and Patterns

Shapes

arch

paisley

lightning

cloud

moon or crescent

fleur-de-lis

spade

diamond

club

heart

smiley face or happy face

musical notes

check

do not sign

Shapes, Symbols, and Patterns

Arrows

up arrow

left arrow

right arrow

down arrow

clockwise arrow

counterclockwise arrow

Shapes, Symbols, and Patterns

Punctuation and Language Symbols

.	?	!	#
dot or period	question mark	exclamation point	pound sign or number sign or hashtag
*	/	@	&
asterisk	slash	at sign	and sign or ampersand
,	'	:	;
comma	apostrophe	colon	semicolon

quotation marks

“	”
open quotation	close quotation

parentheses

(	)
open parenthesis	close parenthesis

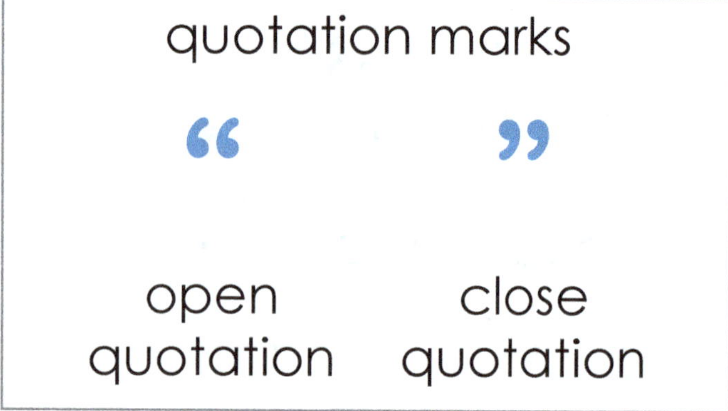

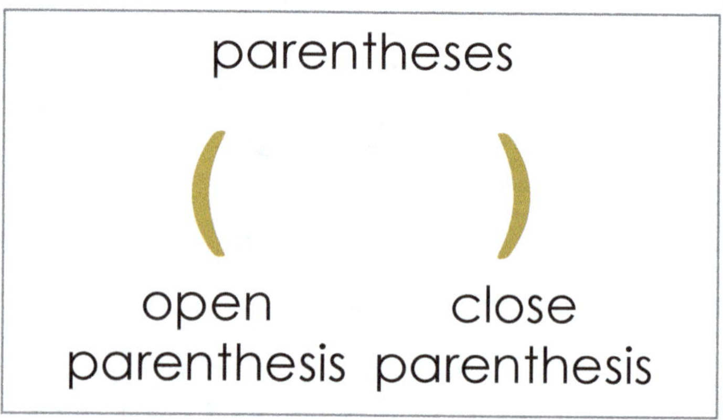

Shapes, Symbols, and Patterns

Mathematical Symbols

Shapes, Symbols, and Patterns

3D Shapes

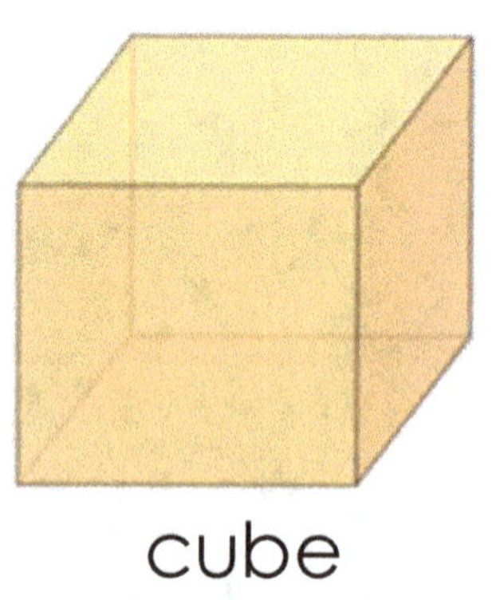
cube

sphere

hemisphere

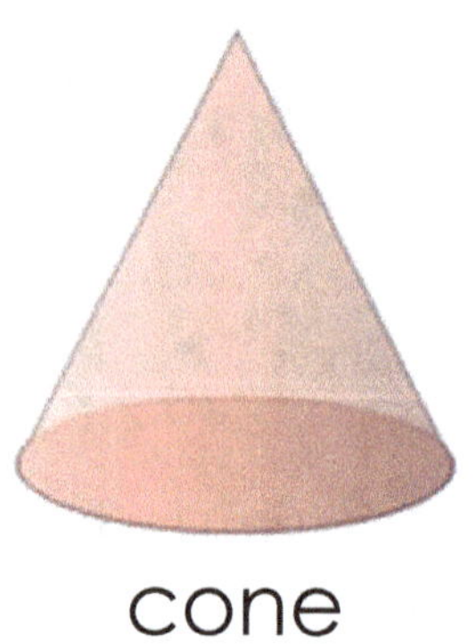
cone

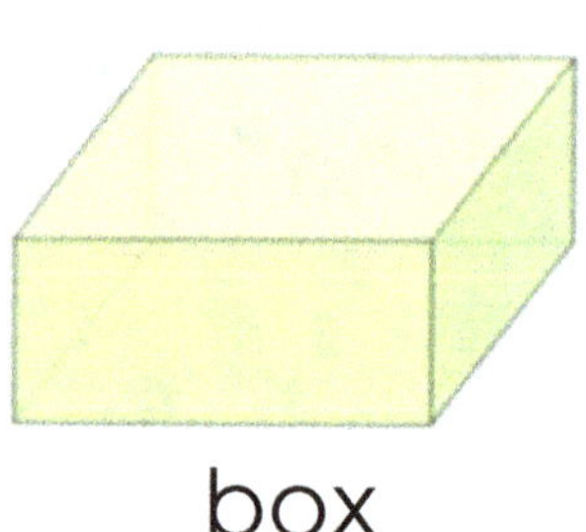
box
or cuboid
or rectangular prism

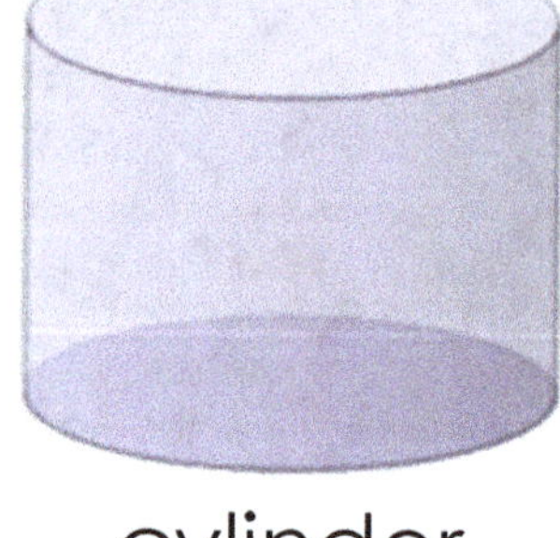
cylinder

donut
or torus

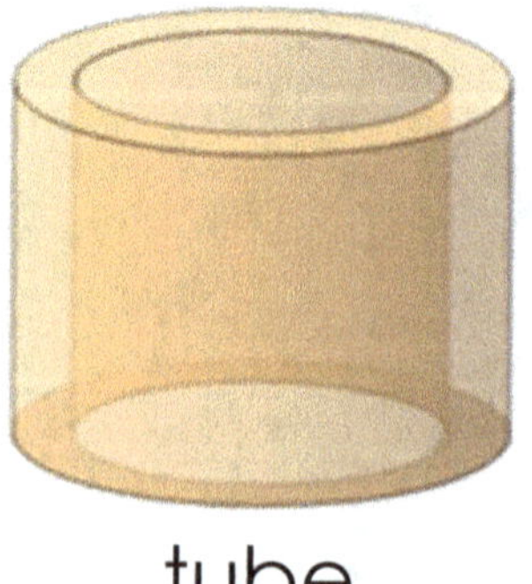
tube
or pipe

egg
or ovoid

Shapes, Symbols, and Patterns

3D Shapes

lens
or bowl

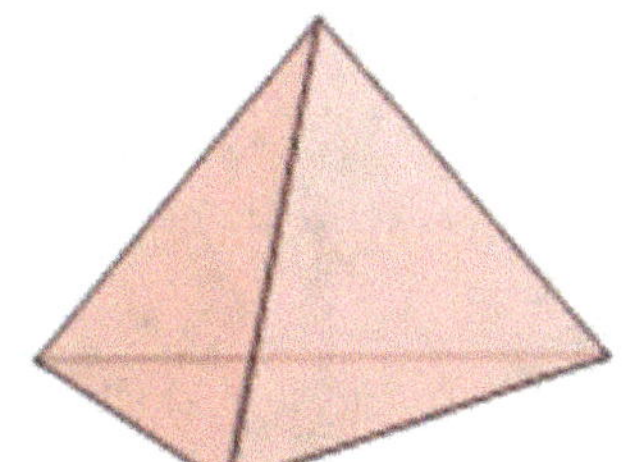

pyramid
or tetrahedron
(4 triangle sides)

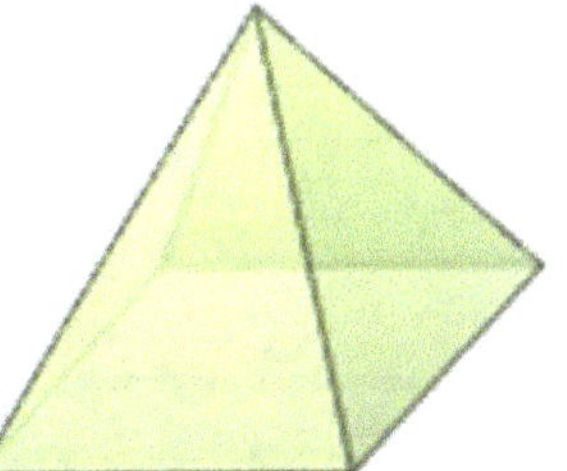

four-sided
pyramid

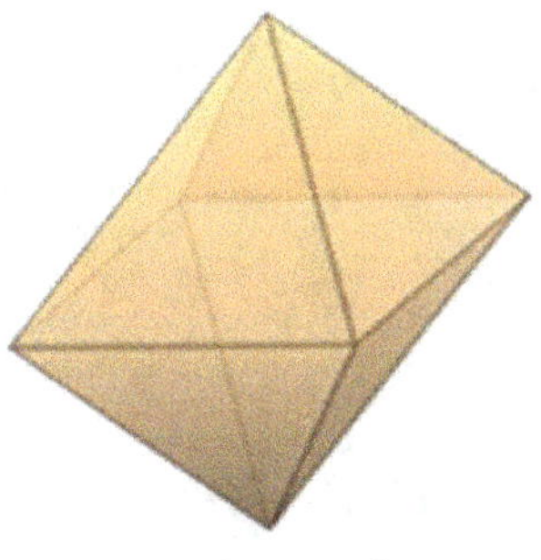

octahedron
(8 triangle sides)

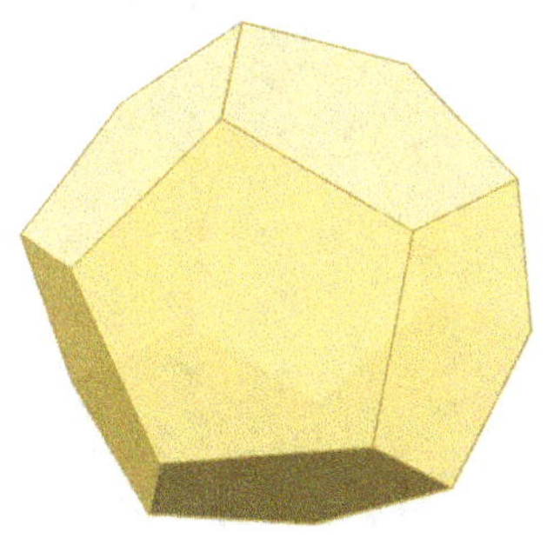

dodecahedron
(12 pentagon sides)

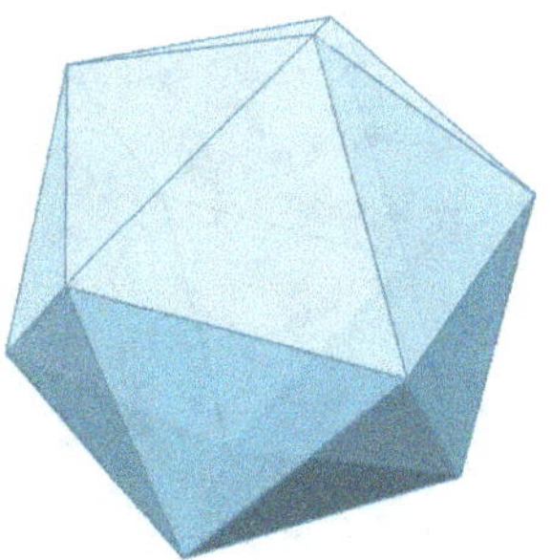

icosahedron
(20 triangle sides)

football

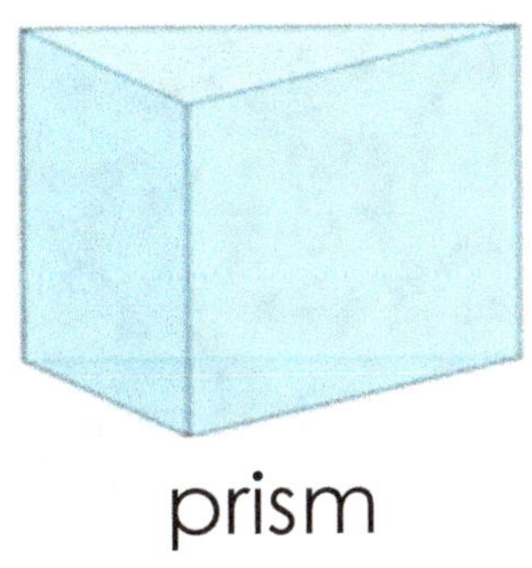

prism

spring
or helix
or coil

bump

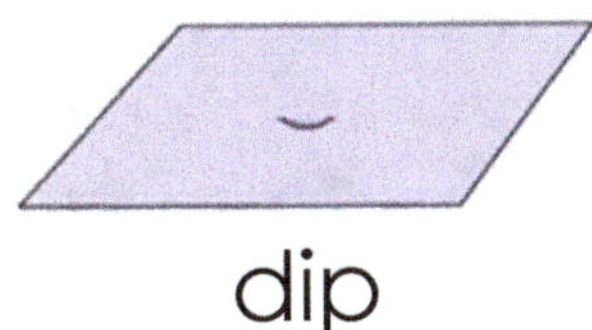

dip

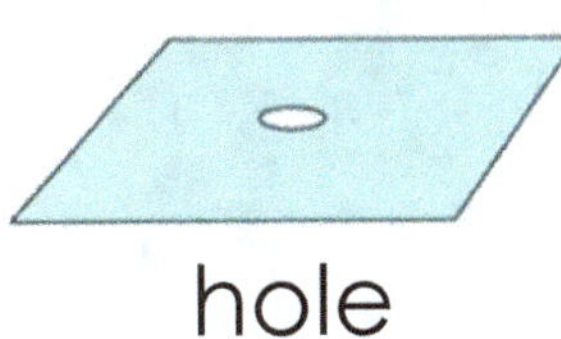

hole

Shapes, Symbols, and Patterns

Lines

horizontal line

vertical line

diagonal lines

parallel lines

intersecting lines

perpendicular lines

straight line

bent line

curved line
or arc

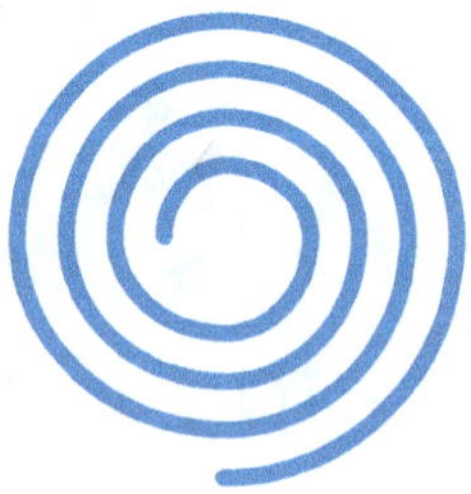

spiral
or curlicue

Shapes, Symbols, and Patterns

Line Patterns

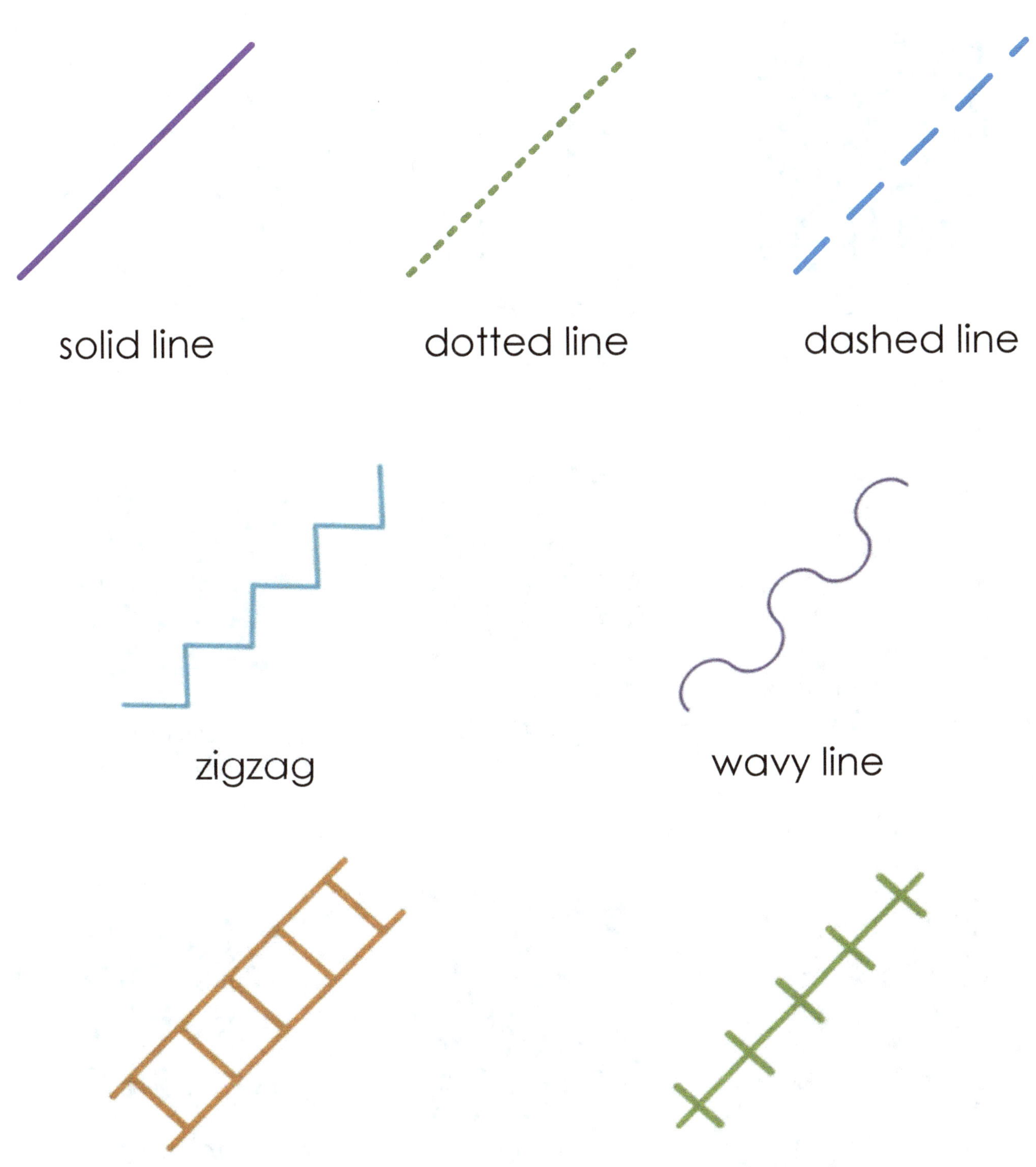

Shapes, Symbols, and Patterns

Area Patterns

solid

stripes

spots

checkers

gingham

plaid

harlequin

lattice

hound's tooth

Shapes, Symbols, and Patterns

Area Patterns

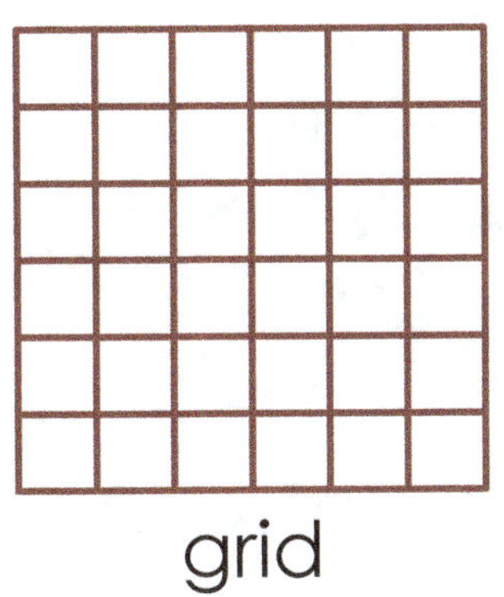

grid

brick

herringbone

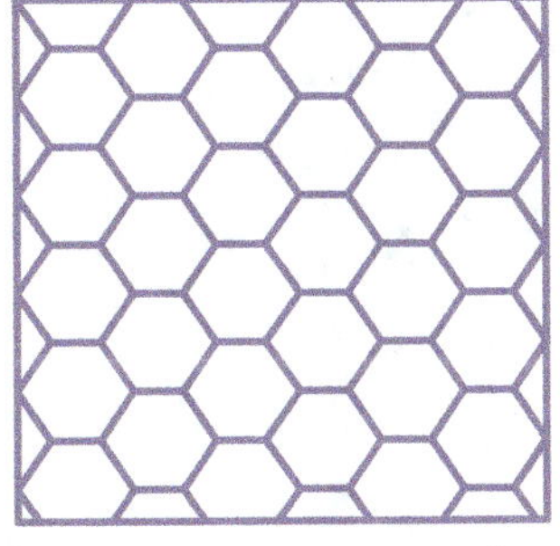

honeycomb

scale

quatrefoil

chevron

basketweave

windowpane

Shapes, Symbols, and Patterns

Area Patterns

animal stripes

animal spots

wood grain

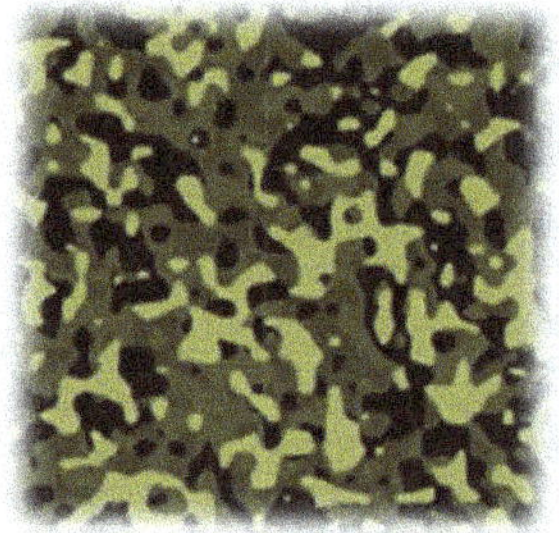

camouflage

Greek key

Celtic knot

Numbers

Numbers

zero	0	
one	1	●
two	2	●●
three	3	●●●
four	4	●●●●
five	5	●●●●●
six	6	●●●●● ●
seven	7	●●●●● ●●
eight	8	●●●●● ●●●
nine	9	●●●●● ●●●●
ten	10	●●●●● ●●●●●

Numbers

eleven	11
twelve	12
thirteen	13
fourteen	14
fifteen	15
sixteen	16
seventeen	17
eighteen	18
nineteen	19
twenty	20

Numbers

twenty-five 25

thirty 30

forty 40

fifty 50

sixty 60

Numbers

Numbers

	1	2	3	4	5	6	7	8	9
10	11	12	13	14	15	16	17	18	19
20	21	22	23	24	25	26	27	28	29
30	31	32	33	34	35	36	37	38	39
40	41	42	43	44	45	46	47	48	49
50	51	52	53	54	55	56	57	58	59
60	61	62	63	64	65	66	67	68	69
70	71	72	73	74	75	76	77	78	79
80	81	82	83	84	85	86	87	88	89
90	91	92	93	94	95	96	97	98	99

Numbers

One Hundred

100

Numbers

One Thousand

1,000

Numbers

Ten Thousand

10,000

Numbers

One Hundred Thousand
100,000

Numbers

Larger Numbers

1	one
10	ten
100	one hundred
1,000	one thousand
10,000	ten thousand
100,000	one hundred thousand
1,000,000	one million
1,000,000,000	one billion
1,000,000,000,000	one trillion

Numbers

Larger Numbers

1,000,000,000,000,000

one quadrillion - 15 zeroes

1,000,000,000,000,000,000

one quintillion - 18 zeroes

1,000,000,000,000,000,000,000

one sextillion - 21 zeroes

1,000,000,000,000,000,000,000,000

one septillion - 24 zeroes

1,000,000,000,000,000,000,000,000,000

one octillion - 27 zeroes

1,000,000,000,000,000,000,000,000,000,000

one nonillion - 30 zeroes

1,000,000,000,000,000,000,000,000,000,000,000

one decillion - 33 zeroes

10,000,000,000,000,000,000,000,000,000,000,000,000,000,000,000,000,000,000,000,000,000,000,000,000,000,000,000,000,000,000,000,000,000,000

one googol - 100 zeroes

Numbers

Ordinals

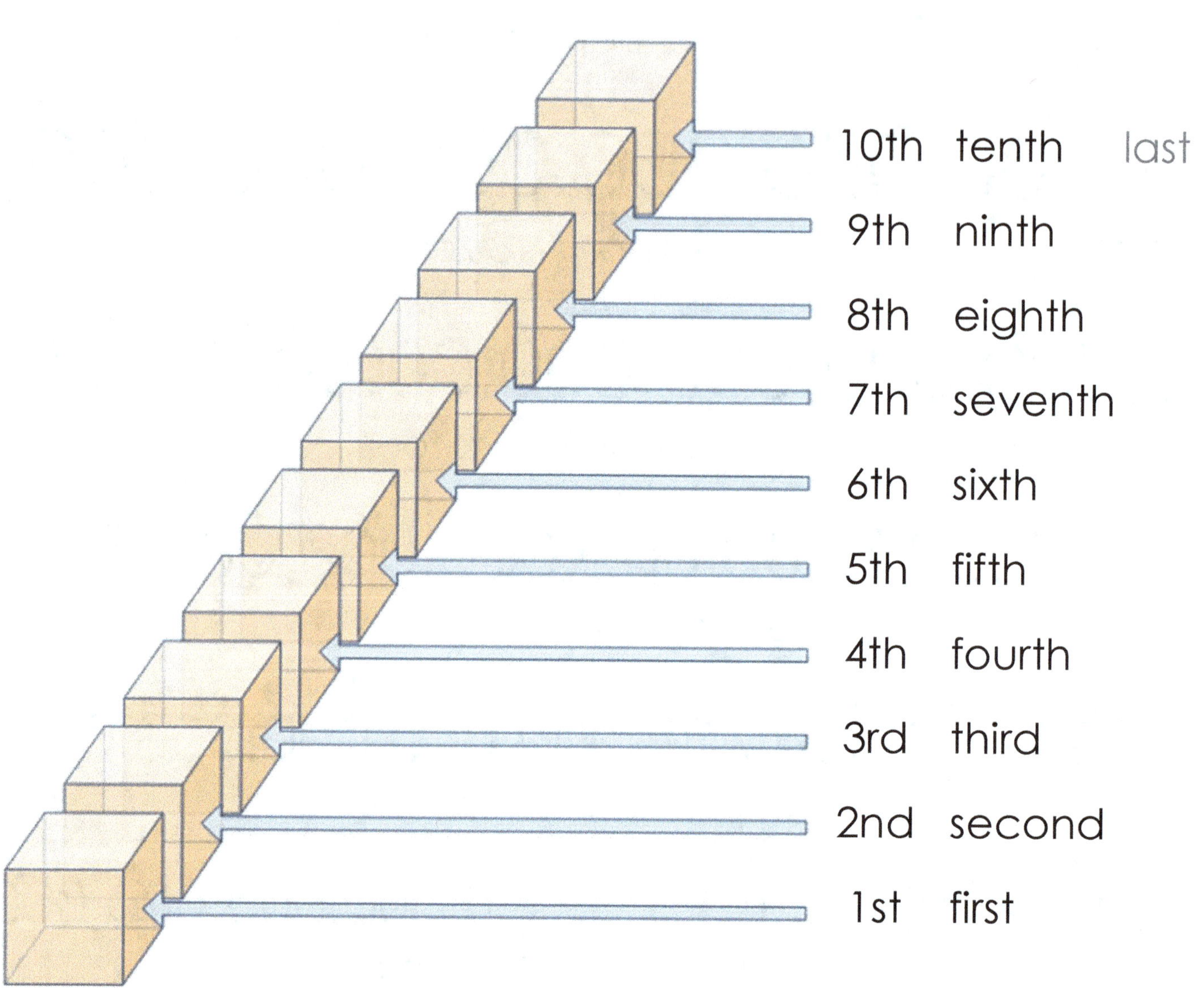

Numbers

Fractions

1/2
one half

Numbers

Fractions

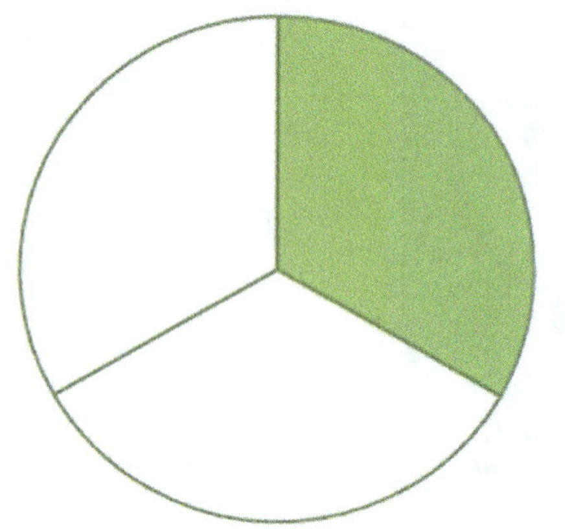

1/3
one third

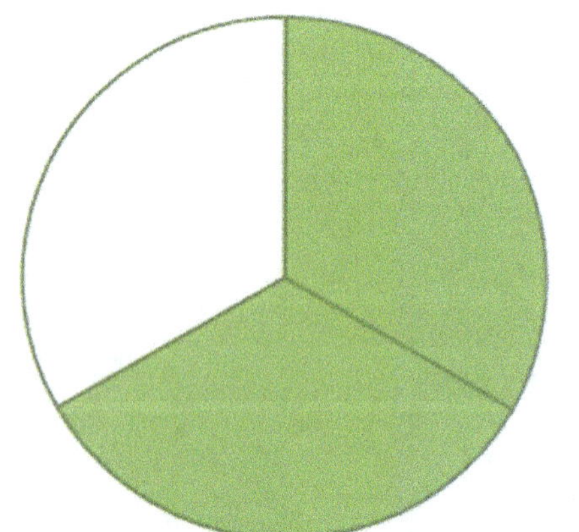

2/3
two thirds

Numbers

Fractions

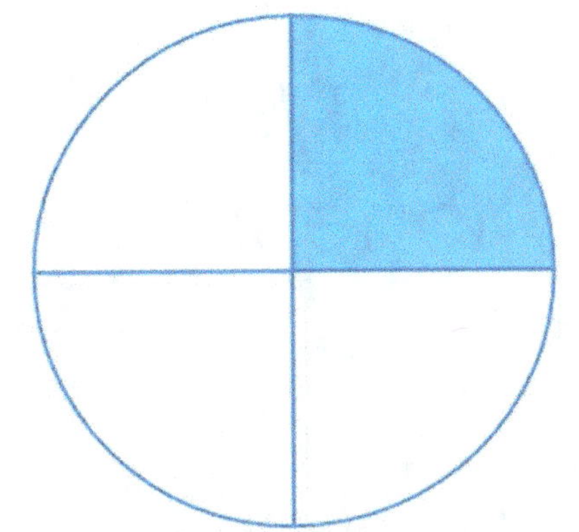

1/4
one fourth
or one quarter

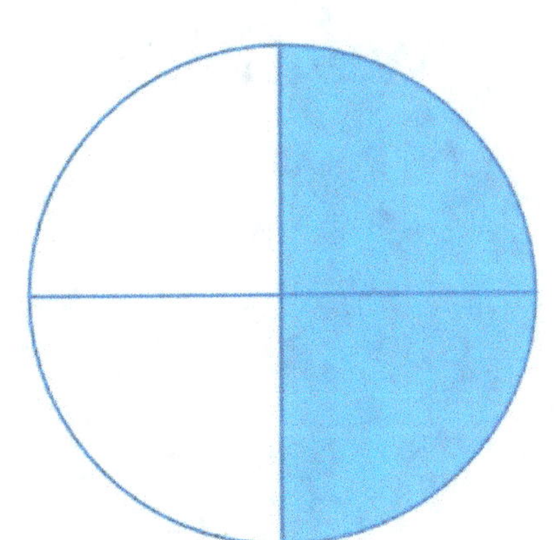

2/4
two fourths
or two quarters

or

1/2
one half

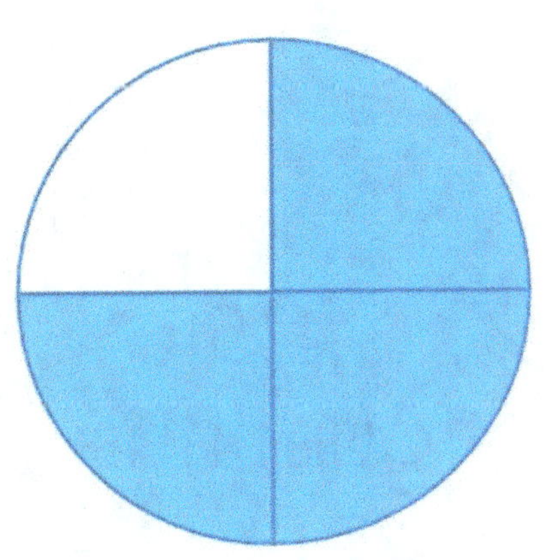

3/4
three fourths
or three quarters

Numbers

Fractions

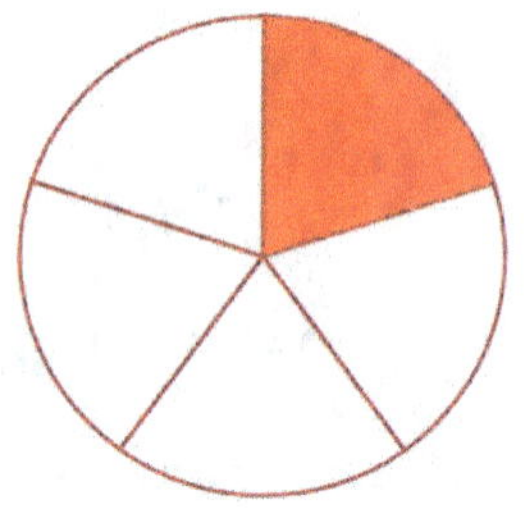

1/5
one fifth

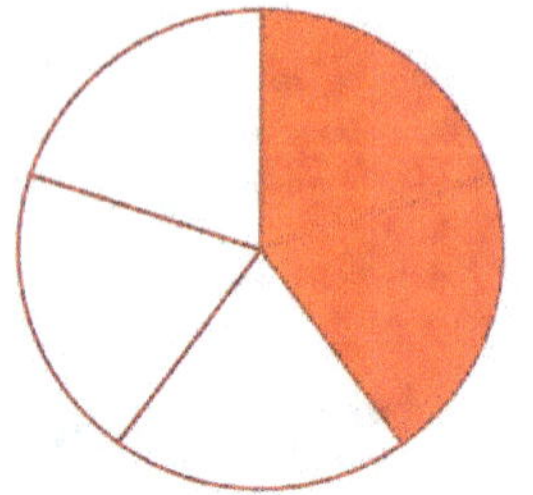

2/5
two fifths

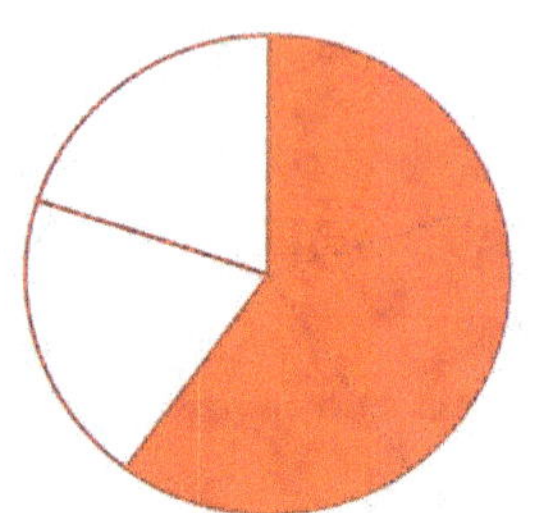

3/5
three fifths

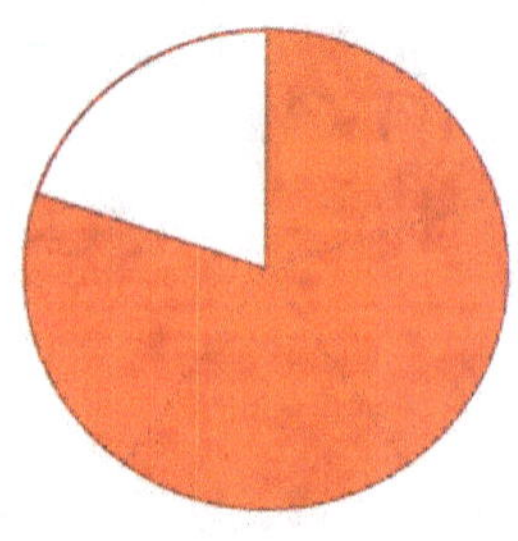

4/5
four fifths

Numbers

Fractions

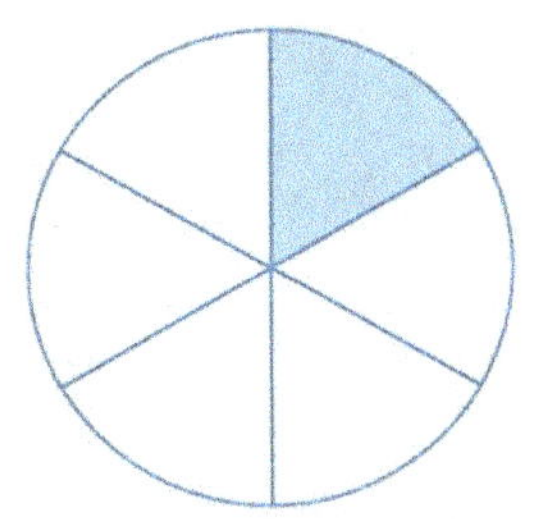

1/6
one sixth

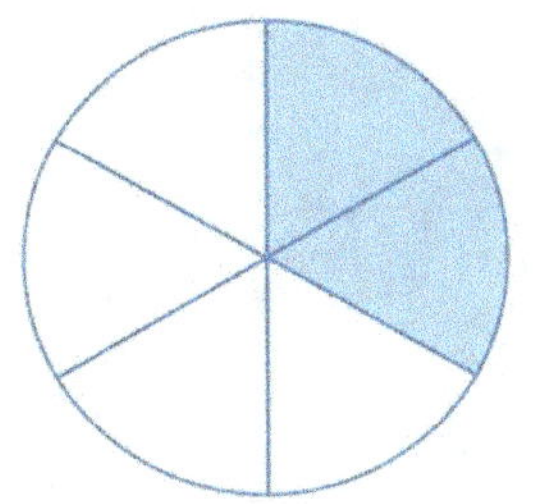
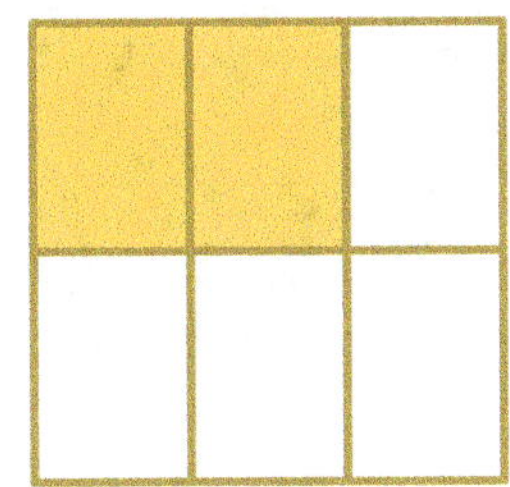

2/6
two sixths

or

1/3
one third

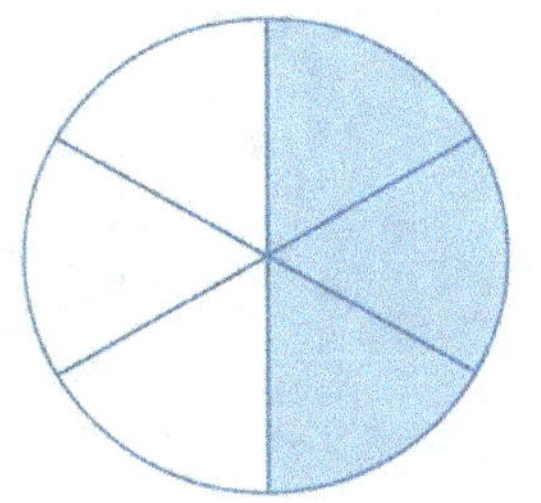
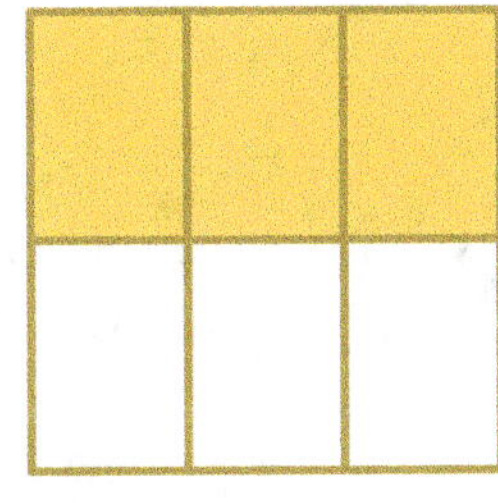

3/6
three sixths

or

1/2
one half

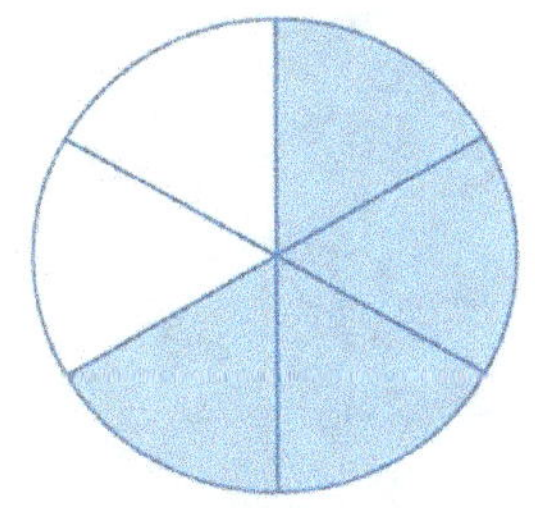
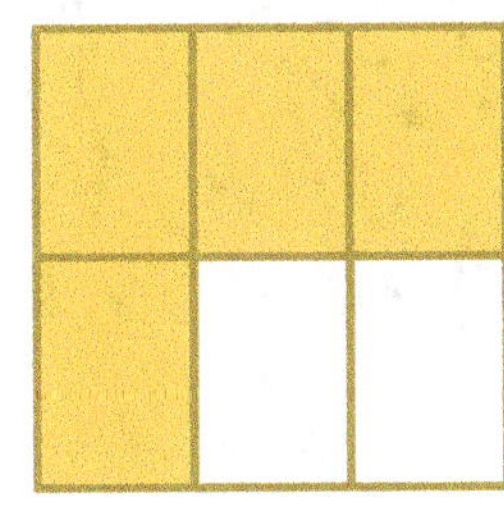

4/6
four sixths

or

2/3
two thirds

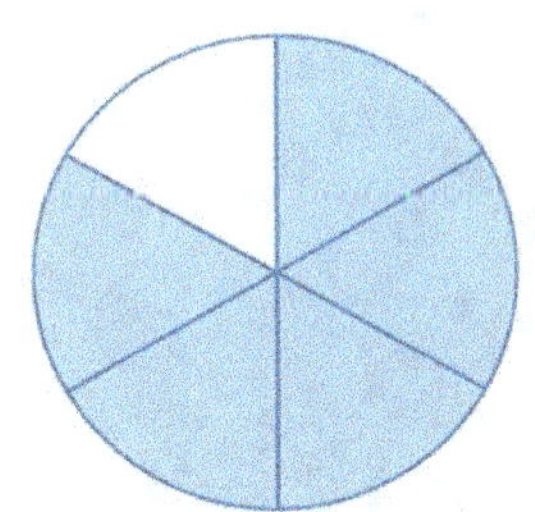
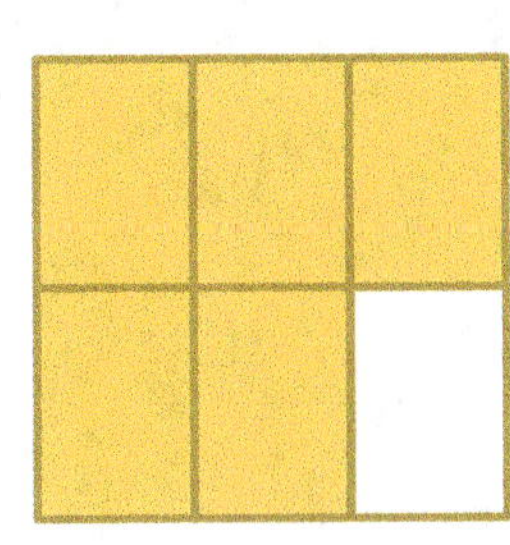

5/6
five sixths

Numbers

Fractions

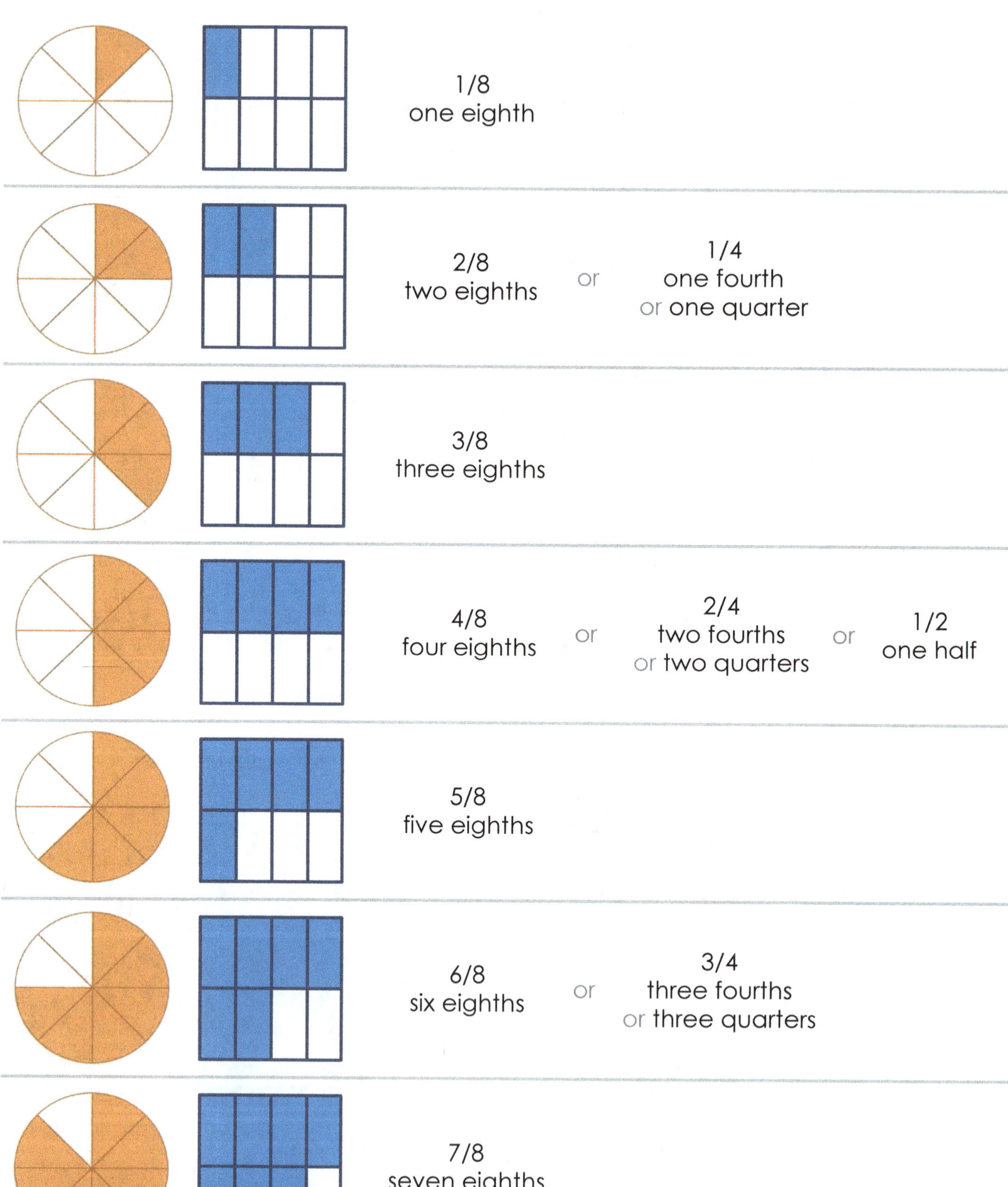

Numbers

Fractions

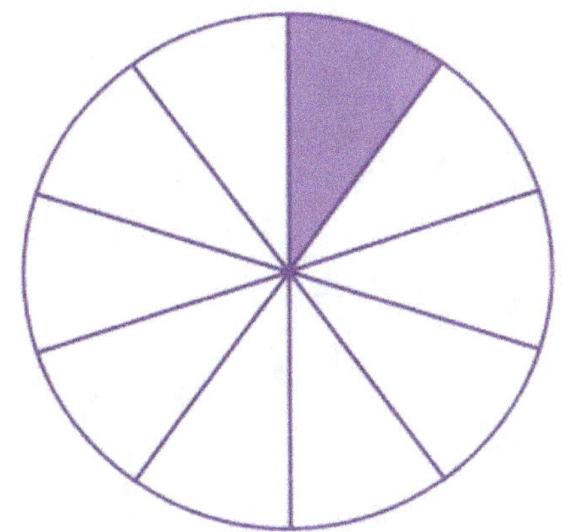

1/10
one tenth

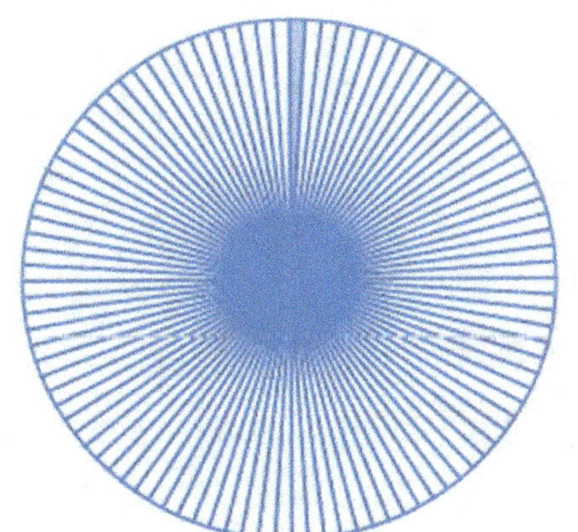

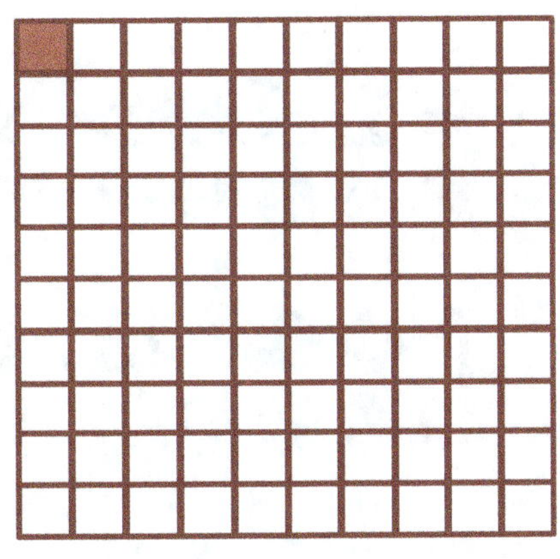

1/100
one hundredth

Numbers

Even Numbers

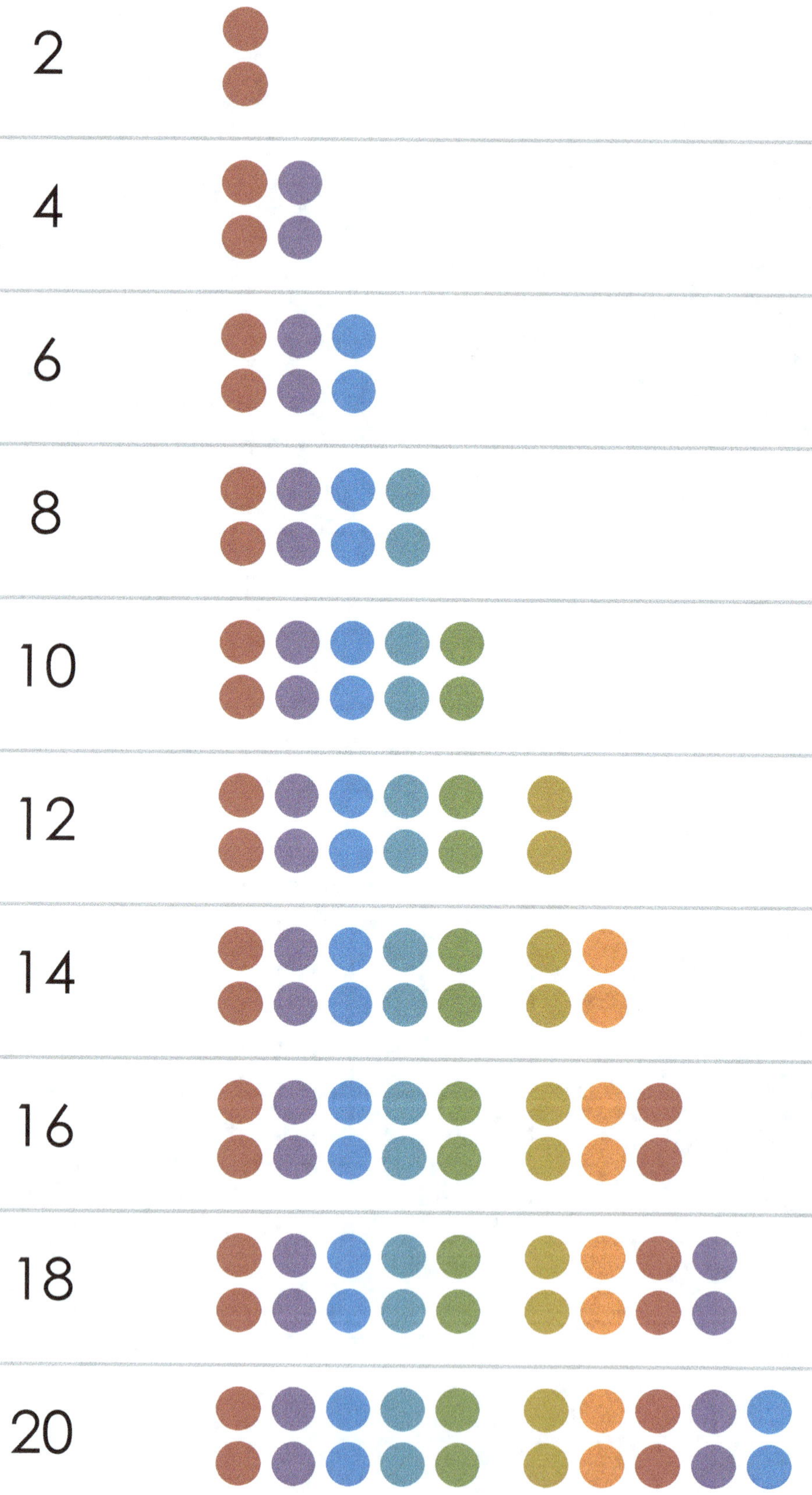

2

4

6

8

10

12

14

16

18

20

Numbers

Odd Numbers

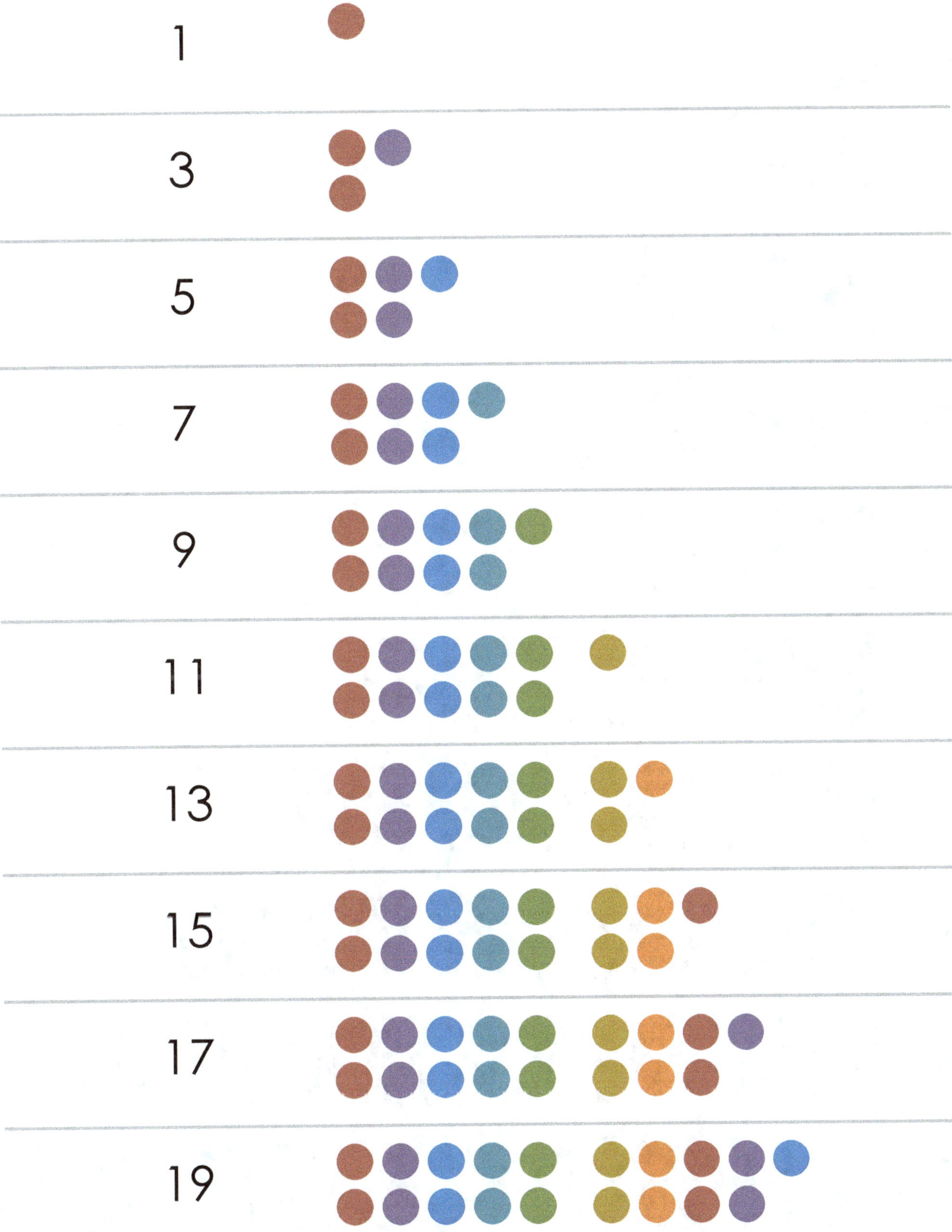

Numbers

Fives

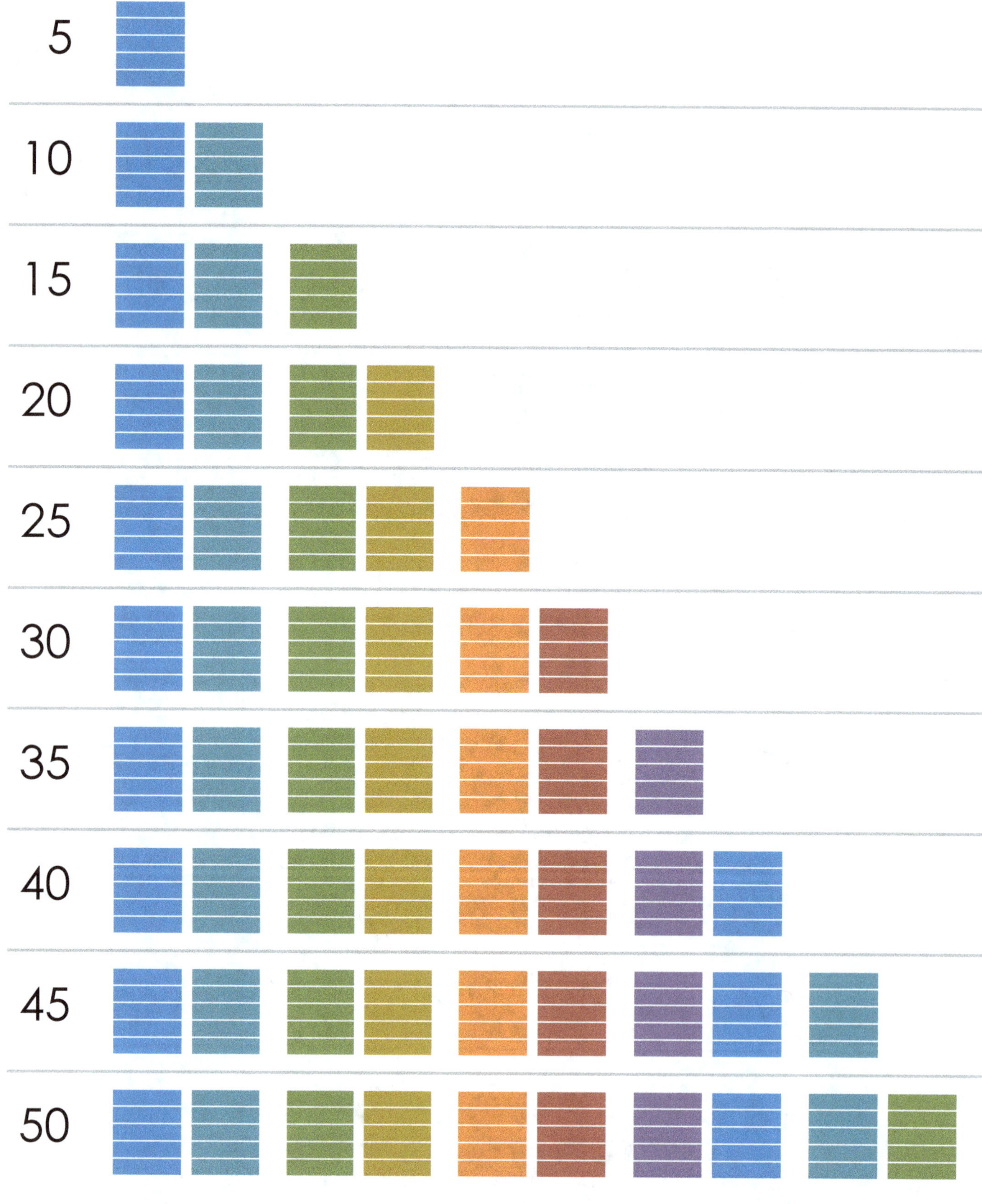

Numbers

Tens

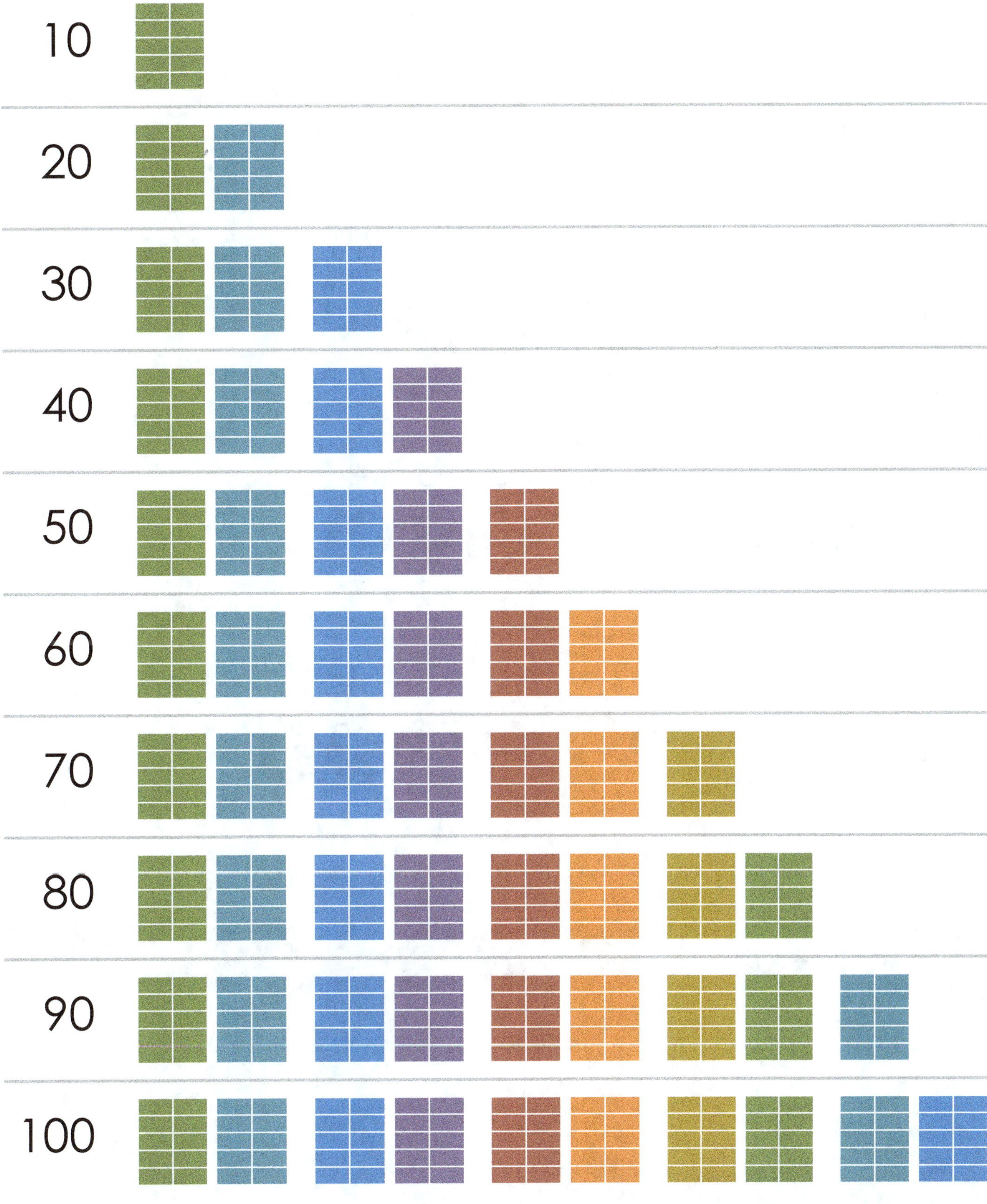

Numbers

Addition

1 + 1 = 2

1 2

1 1

---

1 + 2 = 3

1 2 3

1 1 2

---

1 + 3 = 4

1 2 3 4

1 1 2 3

---

1 + 4 = 5

1 2 3 4 5

1 1 2 3 4

---

1 + 5 = 6

1 2 3 4 5 6

1 1 2 3 4 5

Numbers

Addition

1 2 3

2 + 1 = 3

1 2 1

---

1 2 3 4

2 + 2 = 4

1 2 1 2

---

1 2 3 4 5

2 + 3 = 5

1 2 1 2 3

---

1 2 3 4 5 6

2 + 4 = 6

1 2 1 2 3 4

---

1 2 3 4 5 6 7

2 + 5 = 7

1 2 1 2 3 4 5

Numbers

Addition

1 2 3 4

3 + 1 = 4

1 2 3 1

---

1 2 3 4 5

3 + 2 = 5

1 2 3 1 2

---

1 2 3 4 5 6

3 + 3 = 6

1 2 3 

---

1 2 3 4 5 6 7

3 + 4 = 7

1 2 3 1 2 3 4

---

1 2 3 4 5 6 7 8

3 + 5 = 8

1 2 3 1 2 3 

Numbers

Addition

4 + 1 = 5

1 2 3 4 5

1 2 3 4 1

4 + 2 = 6

1 2 3 4 5 6

1 2 3 4 1 2

4 + 3 = 7

1 2 3 4 5 6 7

1 2 3 4 1 2 3

4 + 4 = 8

1 2 3 4 5 6 7 8

1 2 3 4 1 2 3 4

4 + 5 = 9

1 2 3 4 5 6 7 8 9

1 2 3 4 1 2 3 4 5

Numbers

Addition

1 2 3 4 5 6

5 + 1 = 6 | 1 2 3 4 5 | 1

1 2 3 4 5 6 7

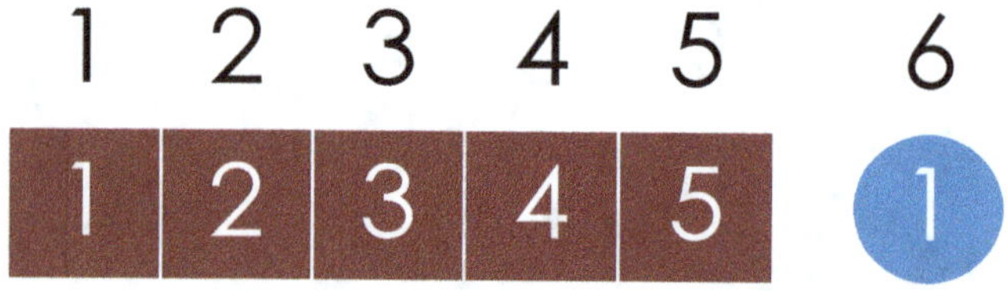

5 + 2 = 7 | 1 2 3 4 5 | 1 2

1 2 3 4 5 6 7 8

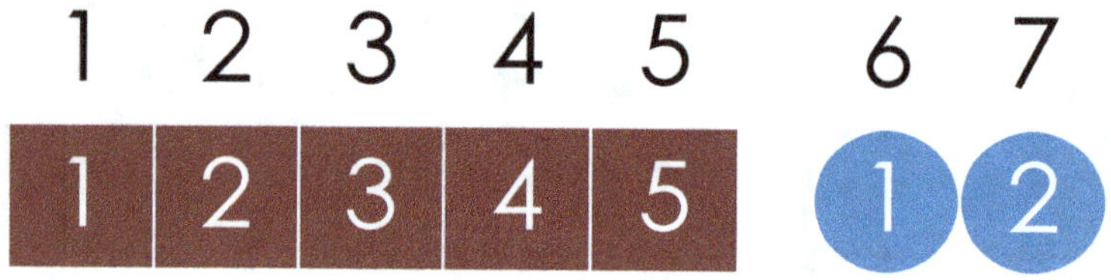

5 + 3 = 8 | 1 2 3 4 5 | 1 2 3

1 2 3 4 5 6 7 8 9

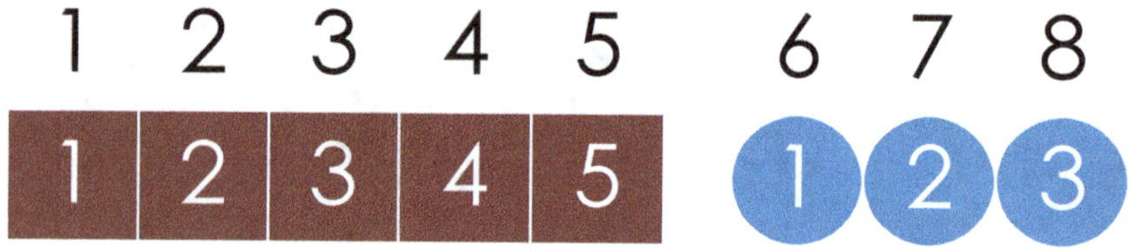

5 + 4 = 9 | 1 2 3 4 5 | 1 2 3 4

1 2 3 4 5 6 7 8 9 10

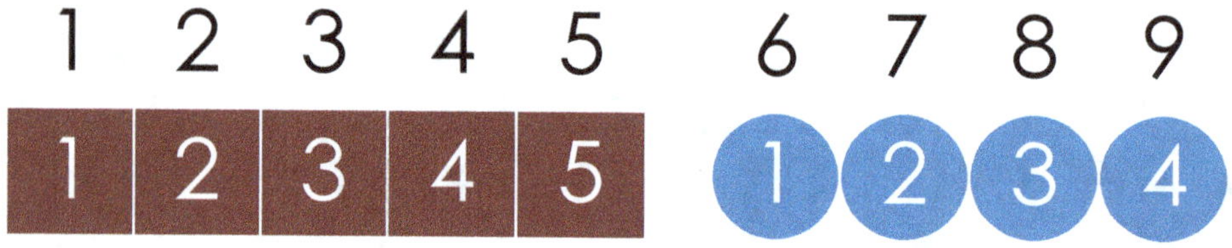

5 + 5 = 10 | 1 2 3 4 5 | 1 2 3 4 5

Numbers

Multiplication

1 x 1 = 1

1 x 2 = 1

2 x 1 = 2

2 x 2 = 4

3 x 1 = 3

3 x 2 = 6

4 x 1 = 4

4 x 2 = 8

5 x 1 = 5

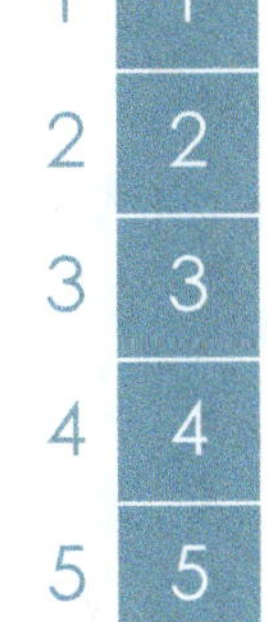

5 x 2 = 10

Numbers

Multiplication

1 x 3 = 3

	1	2	3
1	1	2	3

1 x 4 = 4

	1	2	3	4
1	1	2	3	4

2 x 3 = 6

	1	2	3
1	1	2	3
2	4	5	6

2 x 4 = 8

	1	2	3	4
1	1	2	3	4
2	5	6	7	8

3 x 3 = 9

	1	2	3
1	1	2	3
2	4	5	6
3	7	8	9

3 x 4 = 12

	1	2	3	4
1	1	2	3	4
2	5	6	7	8
3	9	10	11	12

4 x 3 = 12

	1	2	3
1	1	2	3
2	4	5	6
3	7	8	9
4	10	11	12

4 x 4 = 16

	1	2	3	4
1	1	2	3	4
2	5	6	7	8
3	9	10	11	12
4	13	14	15	16

5 x 3 = 15

	1	2	3
1	1	2	3
2	4	5	6
3	7	8	9
4	10	11	12
5	13	14	15

5 x 4 = 20

	1	2	3	4
1	1	2	3	4
2	5	6	7	8
3	9	10	11	12
4	13	14	15	16
5	17	18	19	20

Numbers

Multiplication

1 x 5 = 5

	1	2	3	4	5
1	1	2	3	4	5

---

2 x 5 = 10

	1	2	3	4	5
1	1	2	3	4	5
2	6	7	8	9	10

---

3 x 5 = 15

	1	2	3	4	5
1	1	2	3	4	5
2	6	7	8	9	10
3	11	12	13	14	15

---

4 x 5 = 20

	1	2	3	4	5
1	1	2	3	4	5
2	6	7	8	9	10
3	11	12	13	14	15
4	16	17	18	19	20

---

5 x 5 = 25

	1	2	3	4	5
1	1	2	3	4	5
2	6	7	8	9	10
3	11	12	13	14	15
4	16	17	18	19	20
5	21	22	23	24	25

Numbers

Squares

$1 \times 1 = 1$

$2 \times 2 = 4$

	1	2
1	1	2
2	3	4

$3 \times 3 = 9$

	1	2	3
1	1	2	3
2	4	5	6
3	7	8	9

$4 \times 4 = 16$

	1	2	3	4
1	1	2	3	4
2	5	6	7	8
3	9	10	11	12
4	13	14	15	16

$5 \times 5 = 25$

	1	2	3	4	5
1	1	2	3	4	5
2	6	7	8	9	10
3	11	12	13	14	15
4	16	17	18	19	20
5	21	22	23	24	25

Numbers

Squares

$6 \times 6 = 36$

	1	2	3	4	5	6
1	1	2	3	4	5	6
2	7	8	9	10	11	12
3	13	14	15	16	17	18
4	19	20	21	22	23	24
5	25	26	27	28	29	30
6	31	32	33	34	35	36

$7 \times 7 = 49$

	1	2	3	4	5	6	7
1	1	2	3	4	5	6	7
2	8	9	10	11	12	13	14
3	15	16	17	18	19	20	21
4	22	23	24	25	26	27	28
5	29	30	31	32	33	34	35
6	36	37	38	39	40	41	42
7	43	44	45	46	47	48	49

Numbers

Squares

$8 \times 8 = 64$

	1	2	3	4	5	6	7	8
1	1	2	3	4	5	6	7	8
2	9	10	11	12	13	14	15	16
3	17	18	19	20	21	22	23	24
4	25	26	27	28	29	30	31	32
5	33	34	35	36	37	38	39	40
6	41	42	43	44	45	46	47	48
7	49	50	51	52	53	54	55	56
8	57	58	59	60	61	62	63	64

$9 \times 9 = 81$

	1	2	3	4	5	6	7	8	9
1	1	2	3	4	5	6	7	8	9
2	10	11	12	13	14	15	16	17	18
3	19	20	21	22	23	24	25	26	27
4	28	29	30	31	32	33	34	35	36
5	37	38	39	40	41	42	43	44	45
6	46	47	48	49	50	51	52	53	54
7	55	56	57	58	59	60	61	62	63
8	64	65	66	67	68	69	70	71	72
9	73	74	75	76	77	78	79	80	81

Numbers

Squares

10 x 10 = 100

	1	2	3	4	5	6	7	8	9	10
1	1	2	3	4	5	6	7	8	9	10
2	11	12	13	14	15	16	17	18	19	20
3	21	22	23	24	25	26	27	28	29	30
4	31	32	33	34	35	36	37	38	39	40
5	41	42	43	44	45	46	47	48	49	50
6	51	52	53	54	55	56	57	58	59	60
7	61	62	63	64	65	66	67	68	69	70
8	71	72	73	74	75	76	77	78	79	80
9	81	82	83	84	85	86	87	88	89	90
10	91	92	93	94	95	96	97	98	99	100

Numbers

Cubes

$1 \times 1 \times 1 = 1$

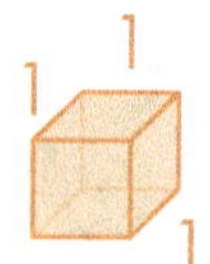

$2 \times 2 \times 2 = 8$

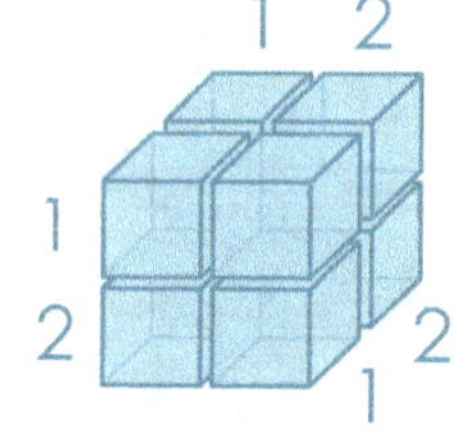

$3 \times 3 \times 3 = 27$

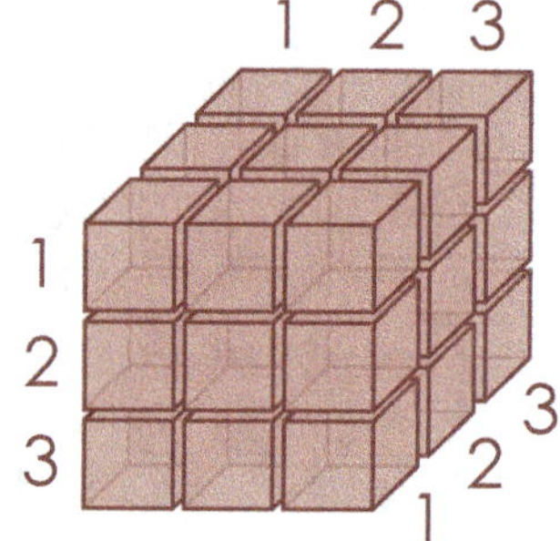

$4 \times 4 \times 4 = 64$

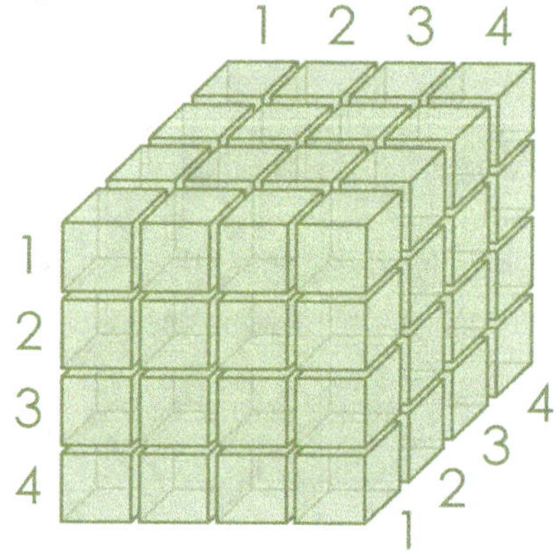

$5 \times 5 \times 5 = 125$

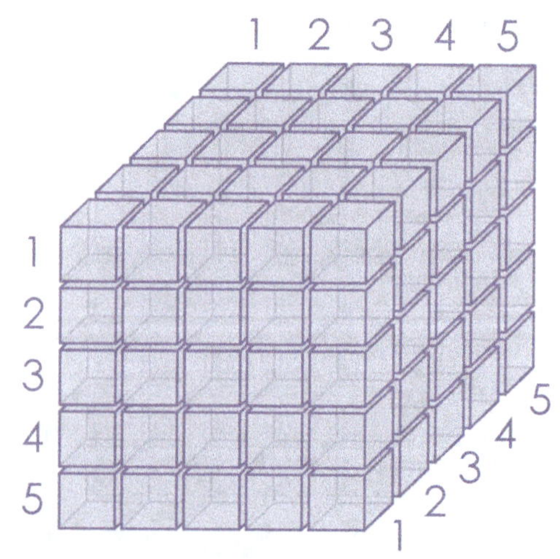

Letters

Letters

A a

A a A a

A a A a

A a A a

A a A a

---

ant	ape	all	arm
cat	face	ball	far
bag	cake	want	part

Letters

B b

B b

B b

B b

B b

B b

B b

B b

B b

---

ball

boy

cub

Letters

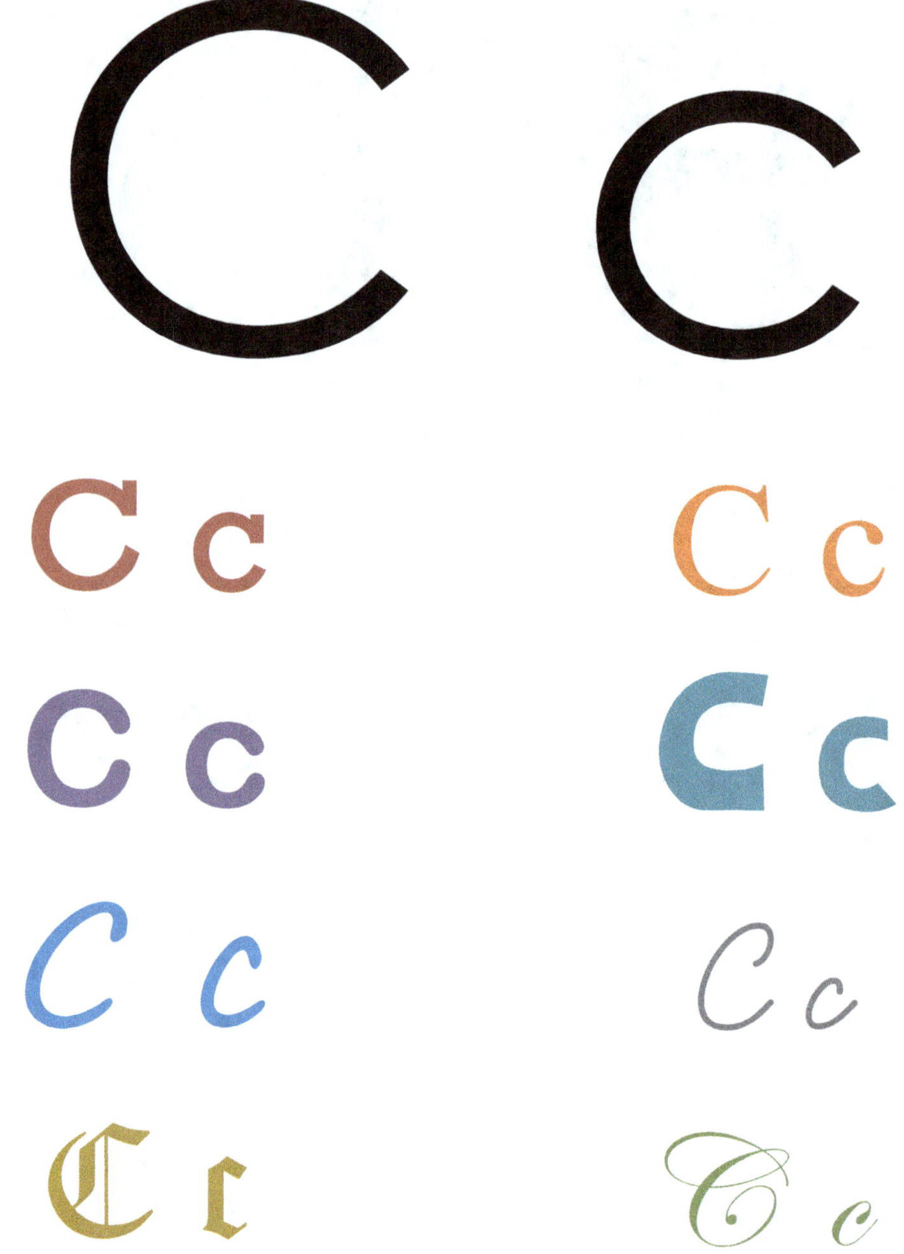

cat
call
act

cell
face
ice

Letters

D d

D d

D d

D d

D d

D d

D d

D d

D d

---

dog

day

mud

Letters

E e

E e

E e

E e

E e

E e

E e

E e

egg
bed
pet

equal
me
see

her
fern
jerk

Letters

F f

F f

F f

F f

F f

F f

F f

F f

F f

---

fun

four

off

of

Letters

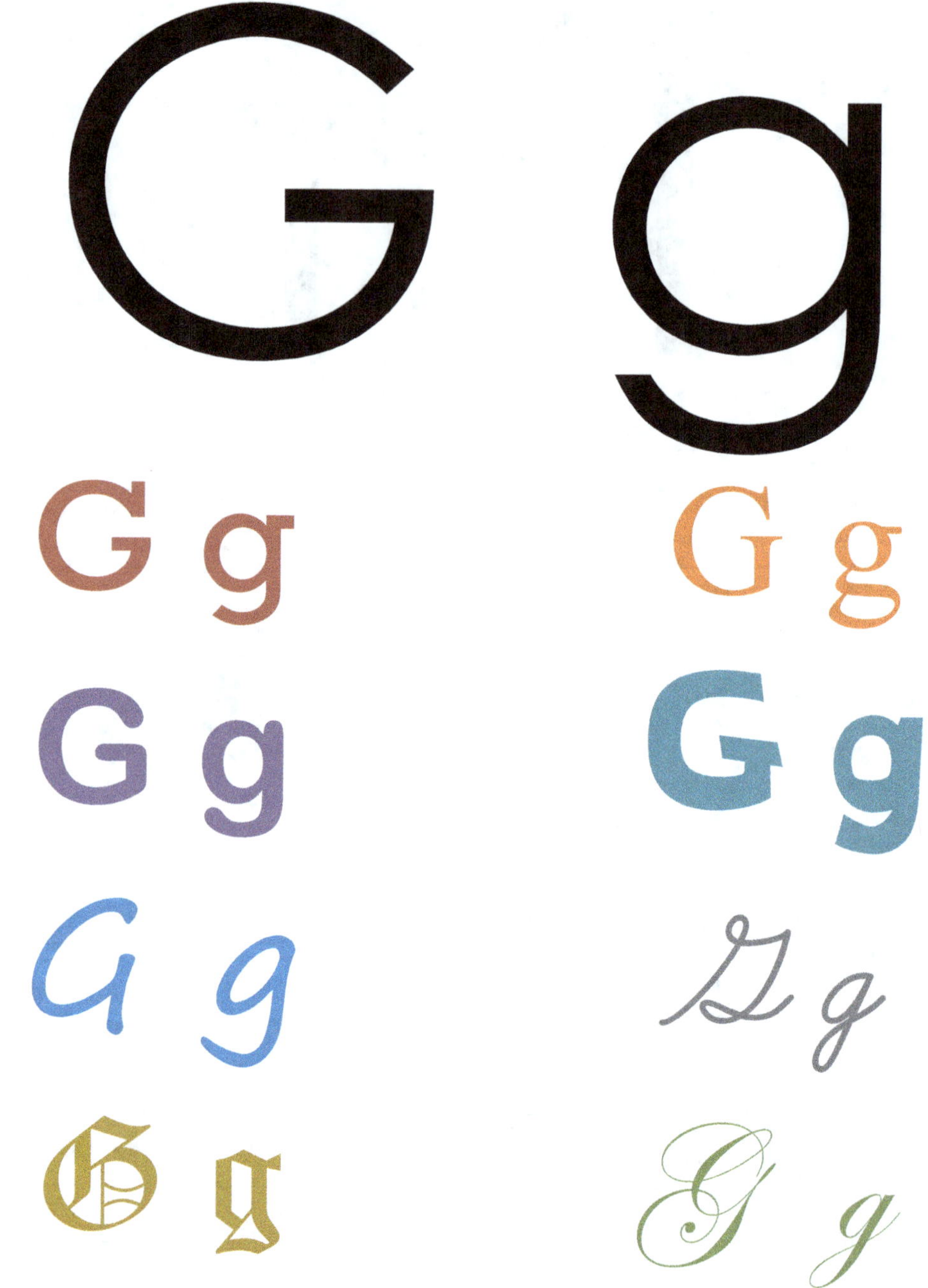

good
girl
dog

gel
gym
age

Letters

H h

H h

H h

H h

H h

H h

H h

H h

H h

---

hot

hay

happy

Letters

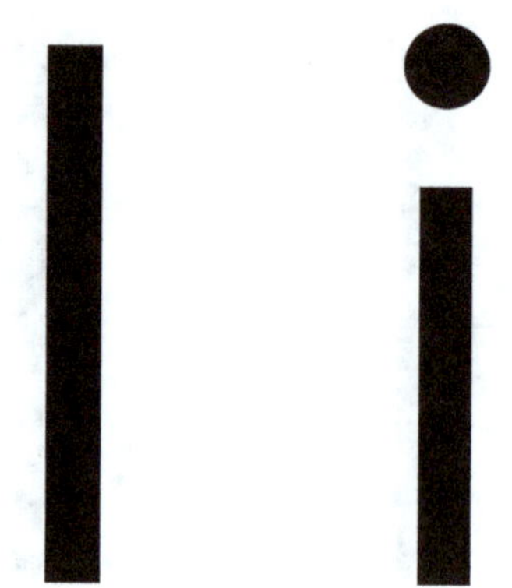

---

in	ice	taxi
hit	lime	kilo
pin	like	piano

Letters

jump

jog

jet

Letters

K k

K k

K k

K k

K k

K k

K k

K k

K k

---

king

lake

cake

Letters

like

late

ball

Letters

M m

M m

M m

M m

M m

M m

M m

M m

M m

may

milk

gum

Letters

N n

N n

N n

N n

N n

N n

N n

N n

N n

---

nap

fan

ten

Letters

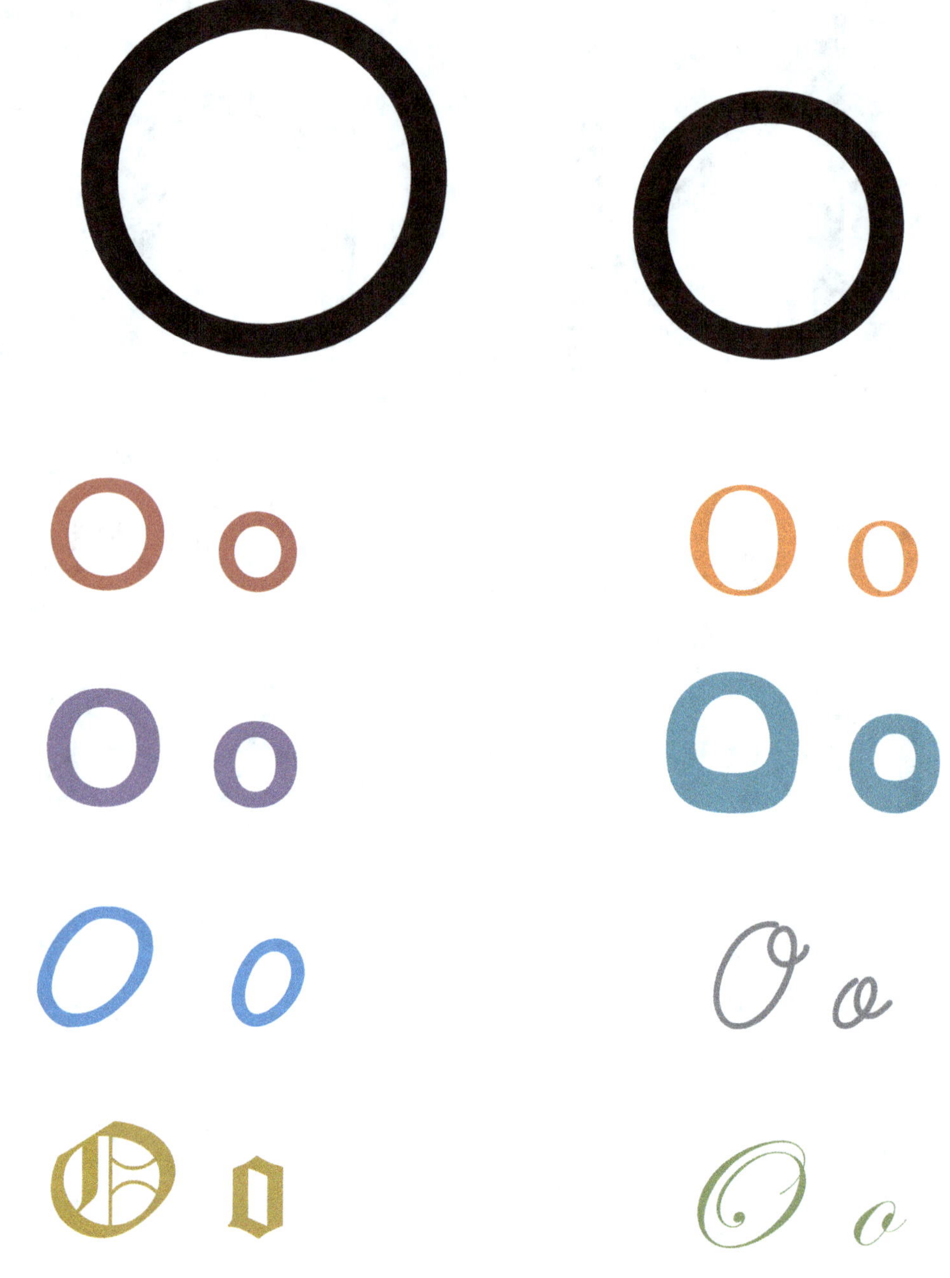

on	open	do	or
hop	rope	two	corn
box	pole	move	fork

Letters

P p

P p

P p

P p

P p

P p

P p

P p

P p

---

pal

tap

ape

Letters

---

quack
quick
squid

unique
plaque

Letters

Rr

Rr Rr

Rr Rr

Rr Rr

Rr Rr

---

run

car

fur

Letters

S s

S s S s

S s S s

S s S s

S s S s

---

say his sure

seven bugs sugar

bus rose

Letters

T t

T t T t

T t T t

T t T t

T t T t

---

top

cat

hot

Letters

U u

U u U u

U u U u

U u U u

U u U u

---

up	tube	use	fur
sun	dune	cute	curl
fun	tune	mule	burn

Letters

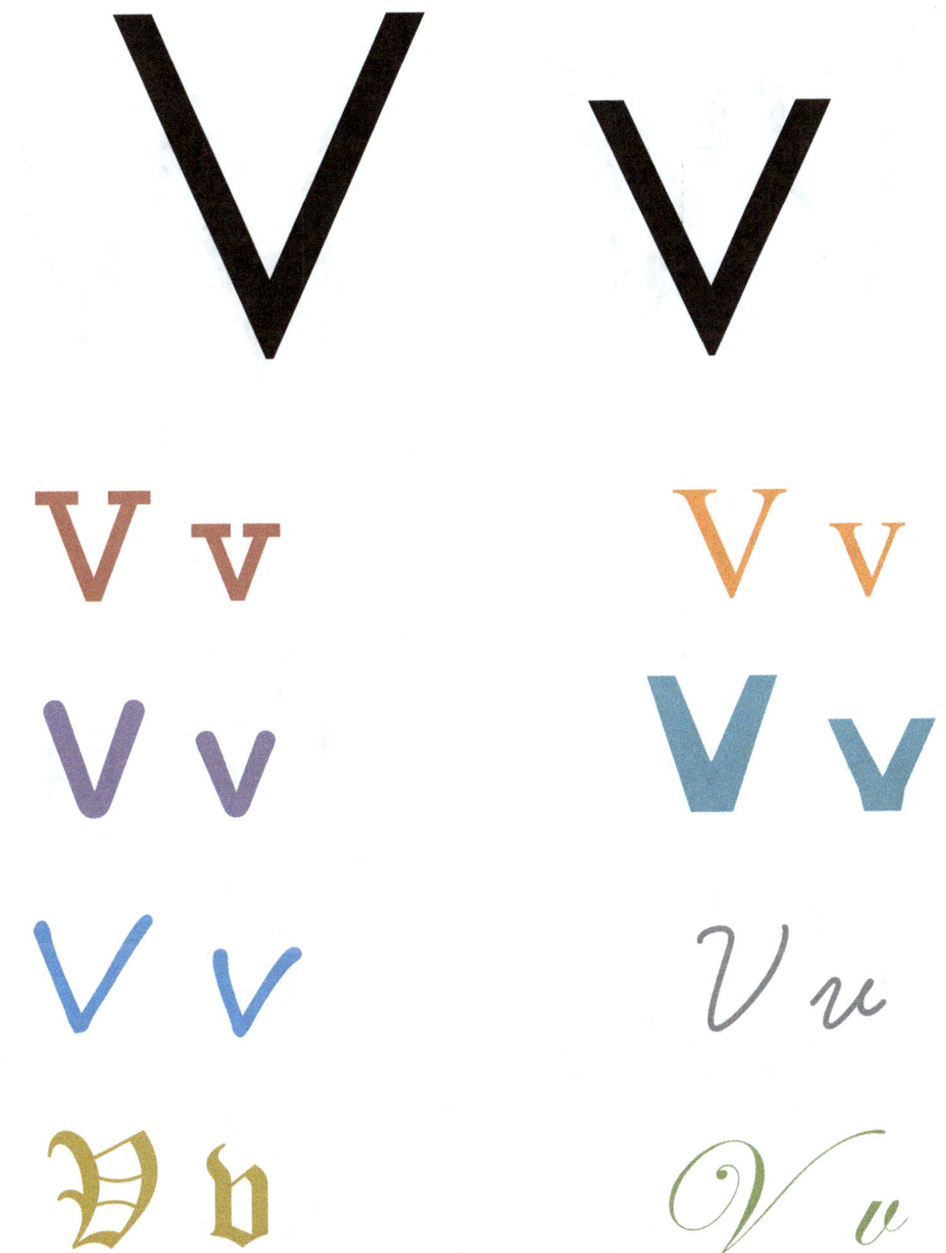

vet

van

five

Letters

want

wet

cow

Letters

box

fox

six

xylophone

Letters

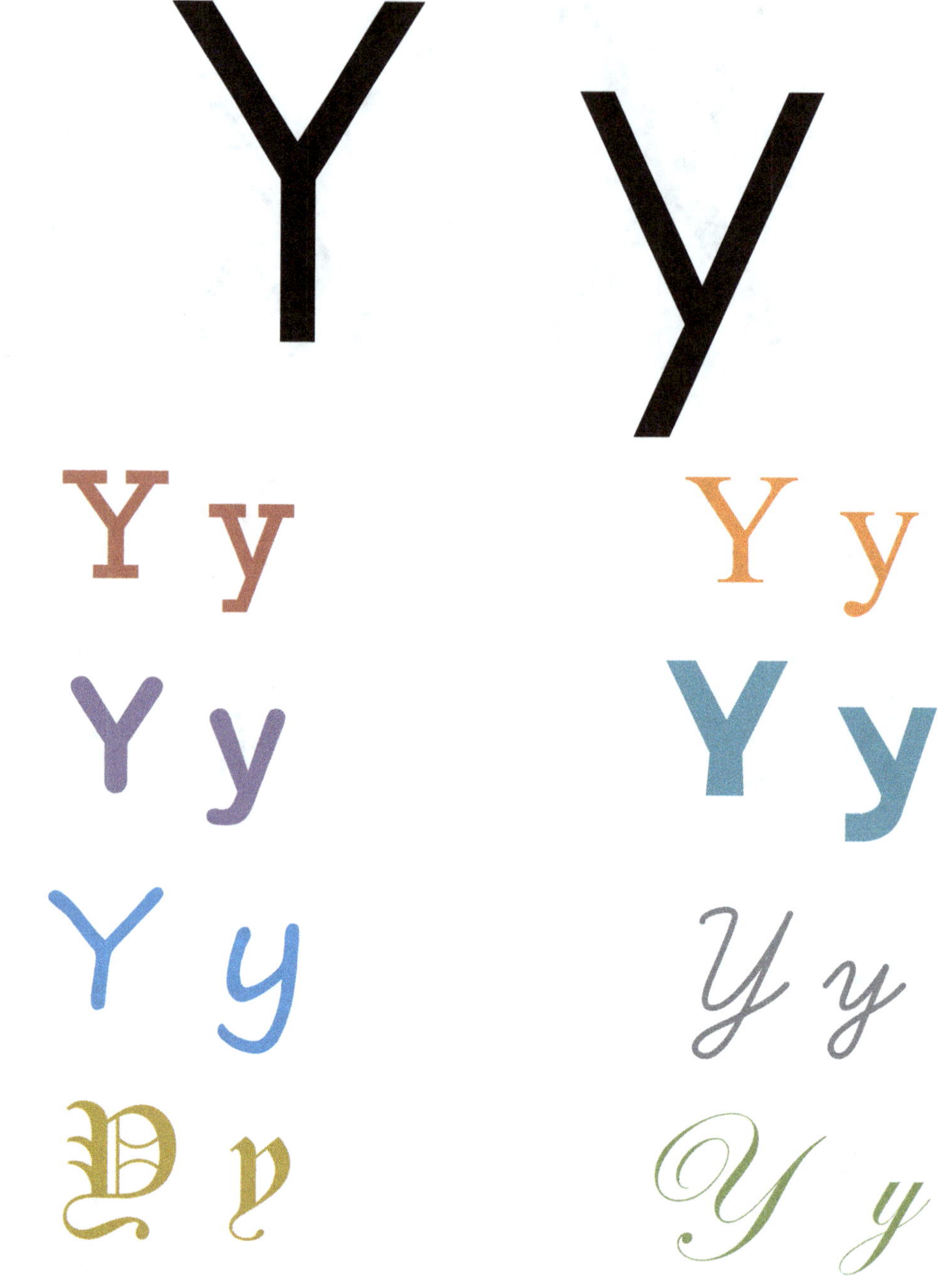

yell
you
yum

by
fly
try

gym

Letters

Z z

Z z

Z z

Z z

Z z

Z z

Z z

Z z

Z z

---

zip

zoom

buzz

Letter Combinations

ch	child chip such	chef
sh	shop shine mush	
th	thin bath with	this that other
ph	phone sphere graph	
ng	thing long rang	finger hungry bongo
gh	laugh tough cough	though dough through

Letter Combinations

oo	boot moo tool	cook foot look
ou	out loud sour	you soup group
oi	oil coil join	
oy	boy toy joy	
ow	cow down brown	mow low bowl
silent e	bit cap not cub	bite cape note cube

Body Parts

Body Parts

Body

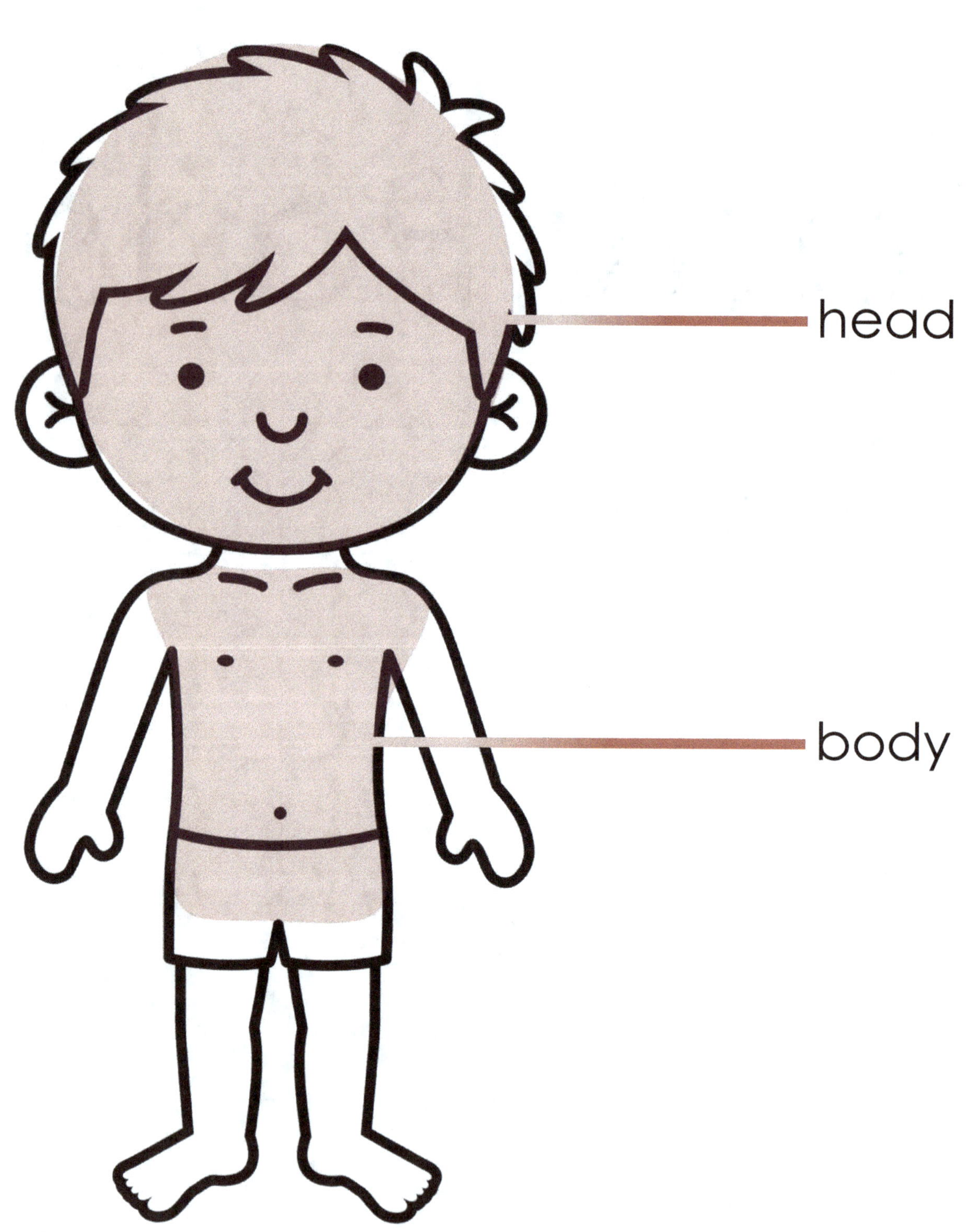

Body Parts

Body

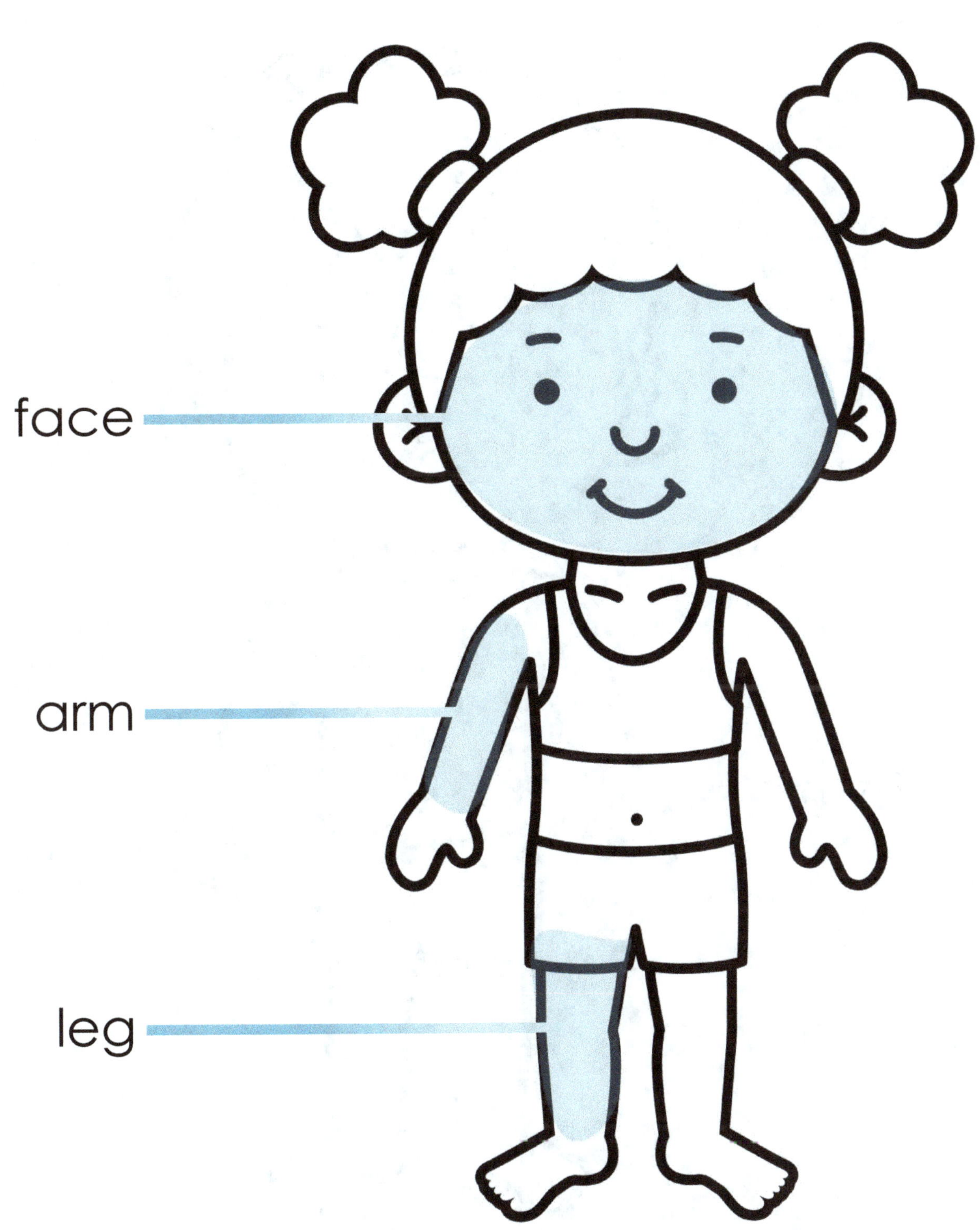

Body Parts

Body

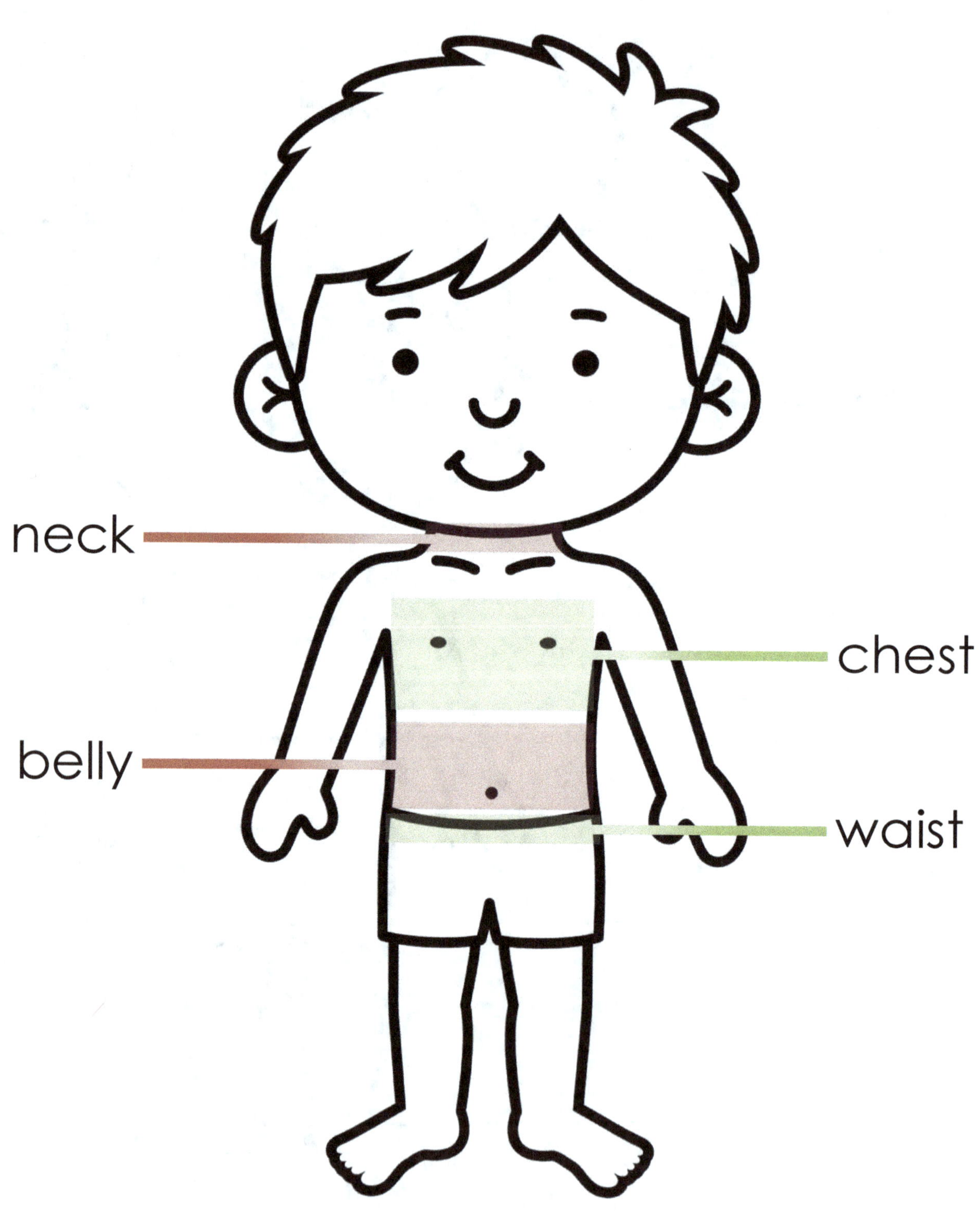

Body Parts

Body

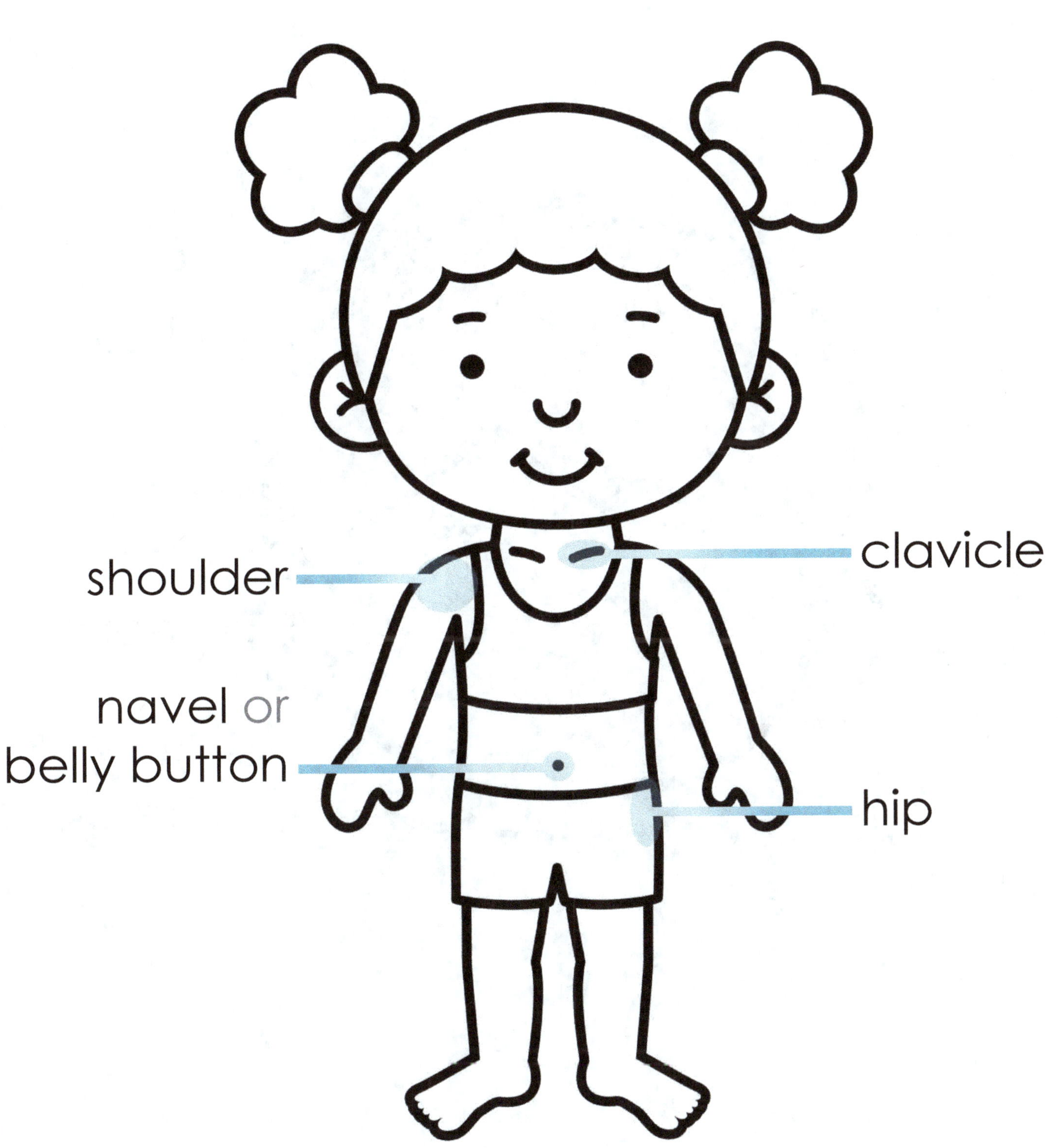

Body Parts

Head and Face

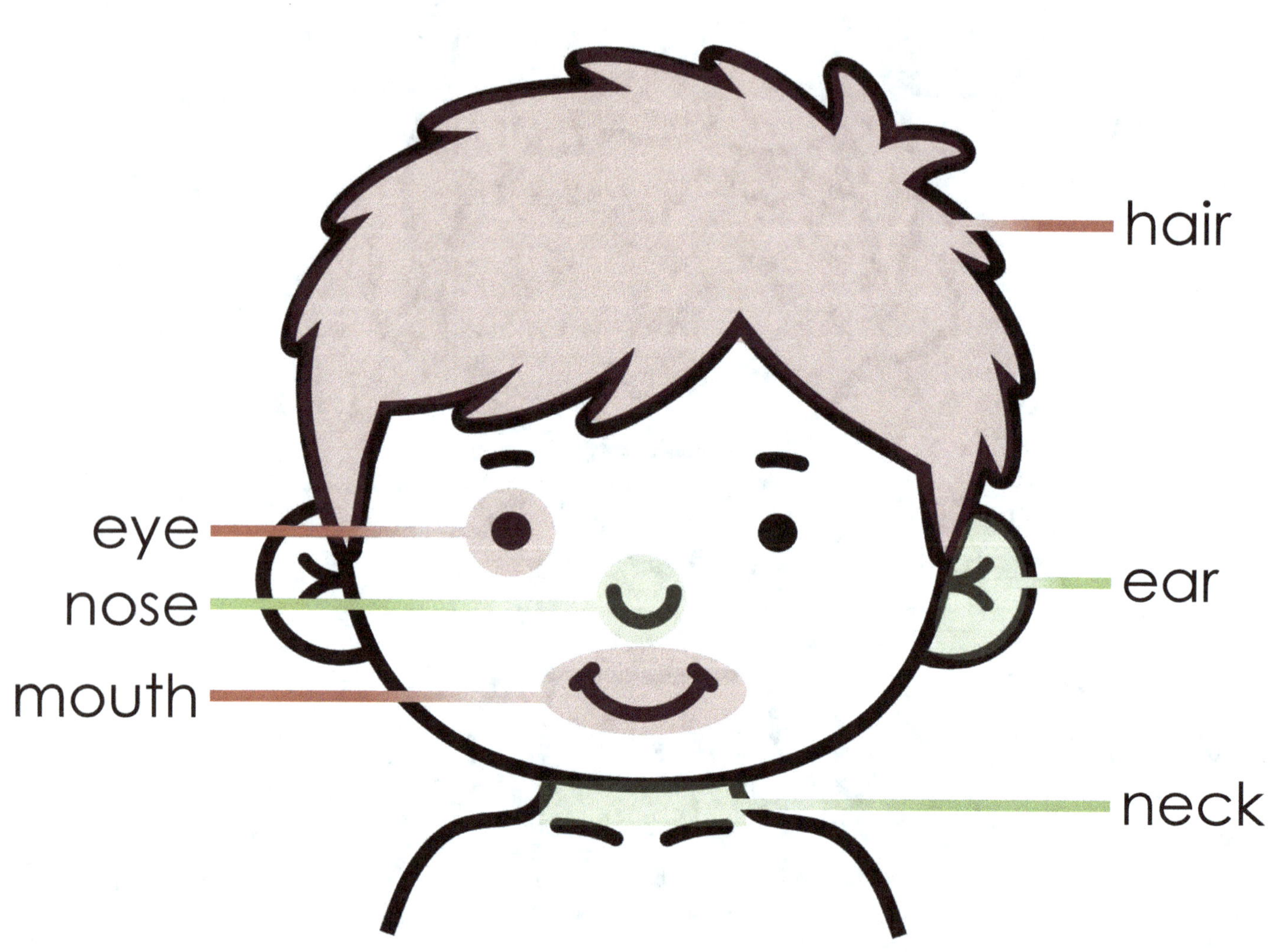

Body Parts

Head and Face

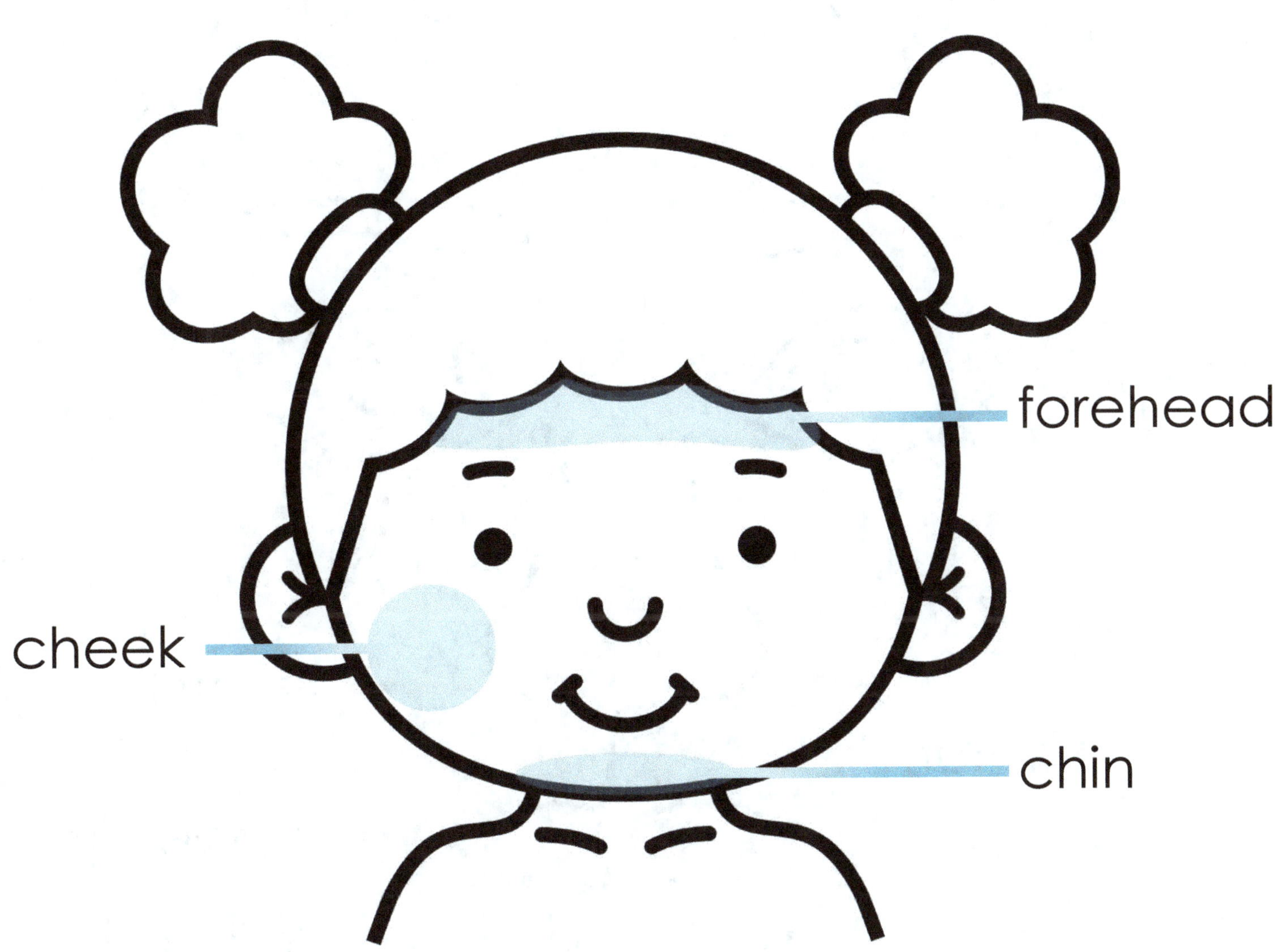

Body Parts

Head and Face

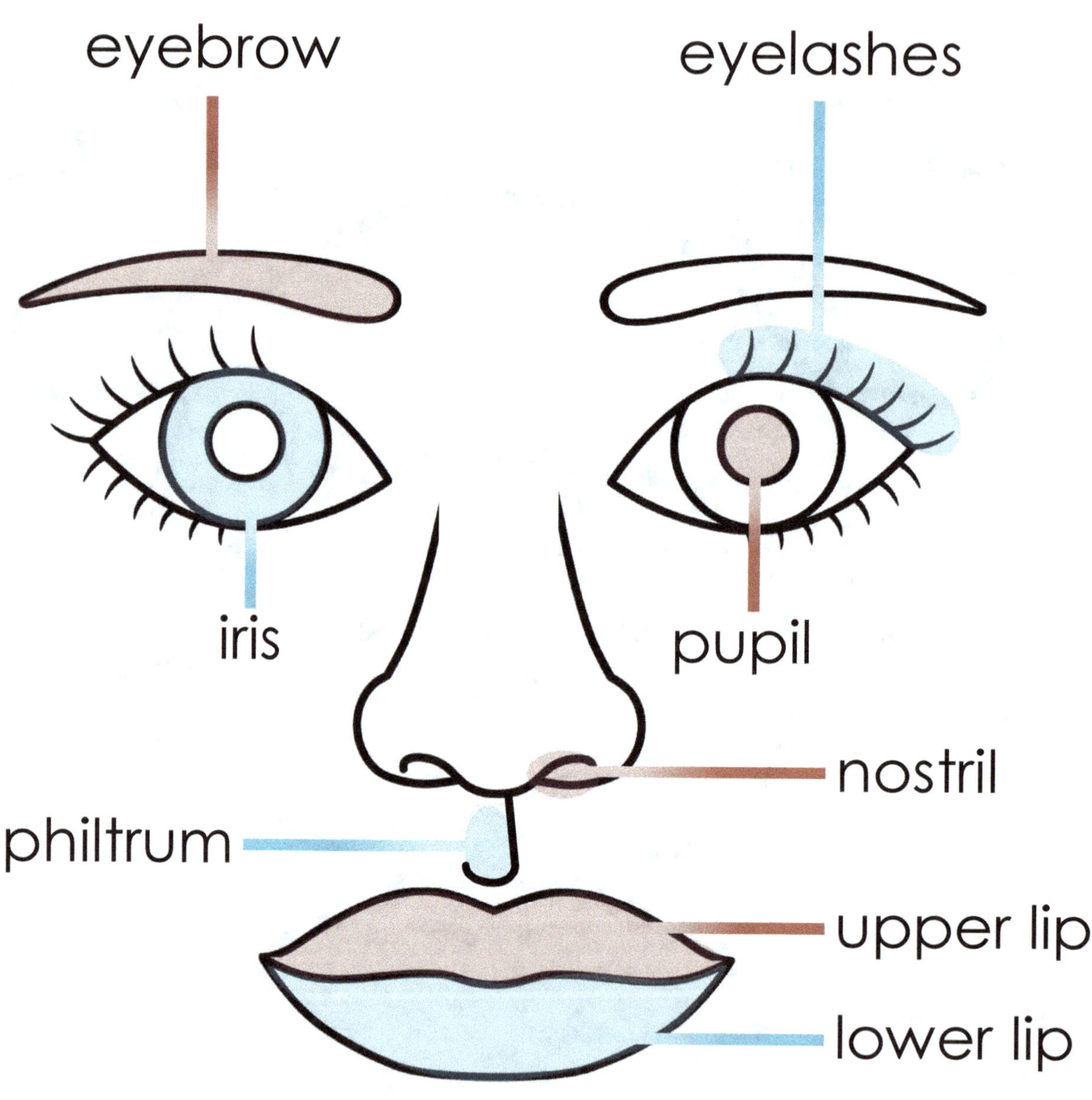

Body Parts

Head and Face

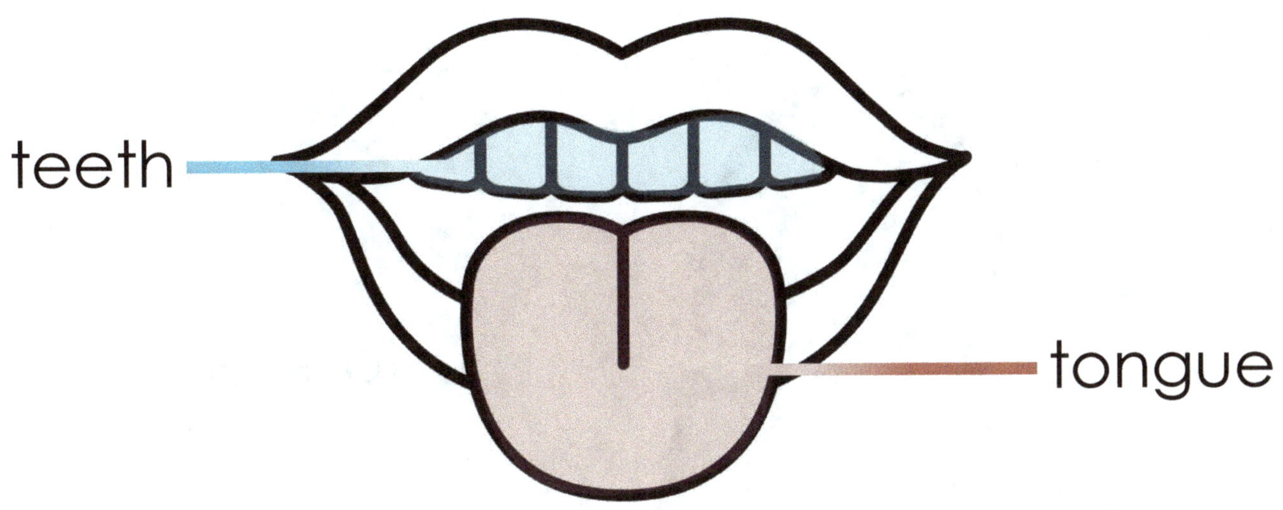

Body Parts

Arm and Hand

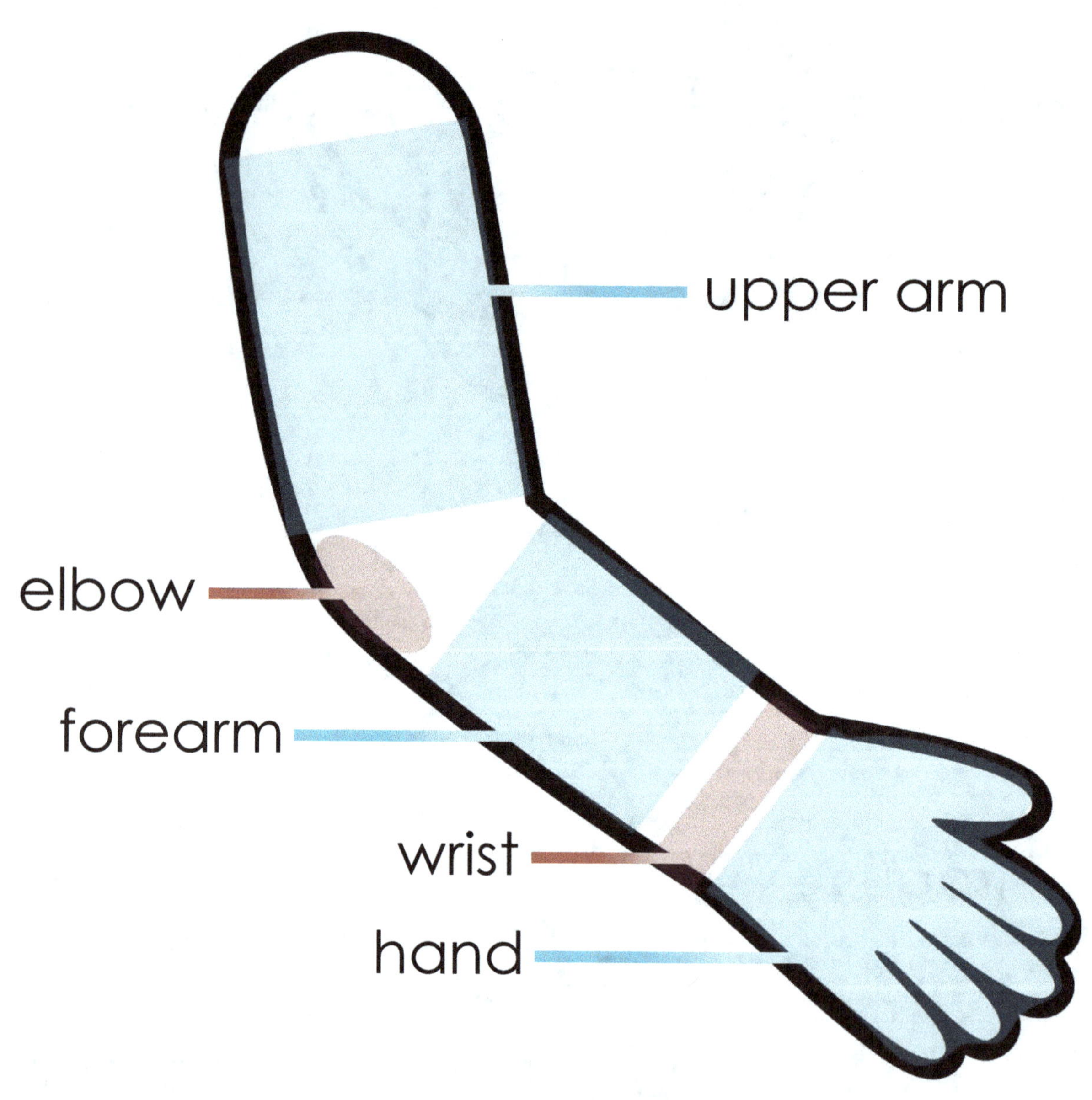

Body Parts

Hands

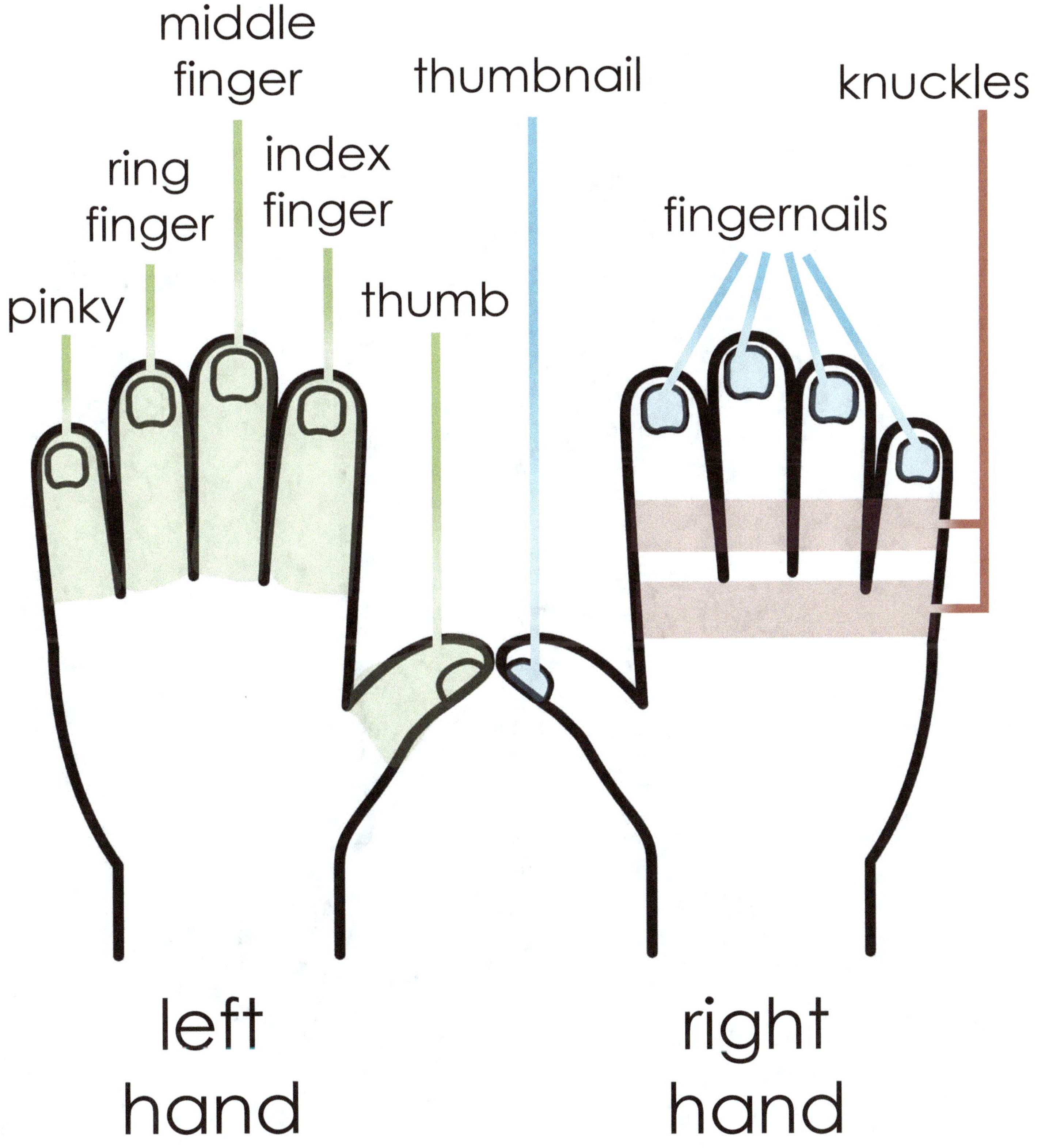

Body Parts

Leg and Foot

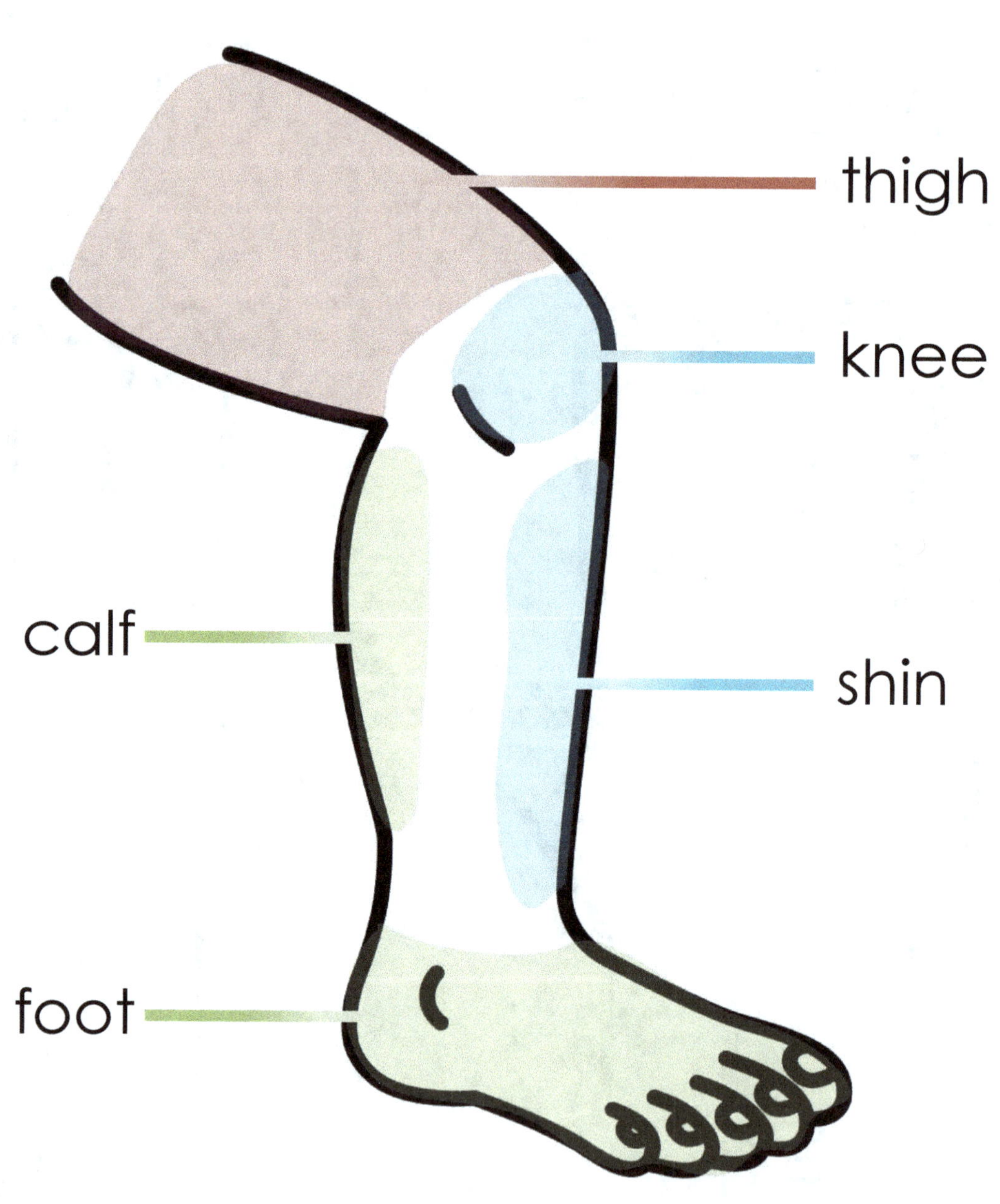

Body Parts

Foot

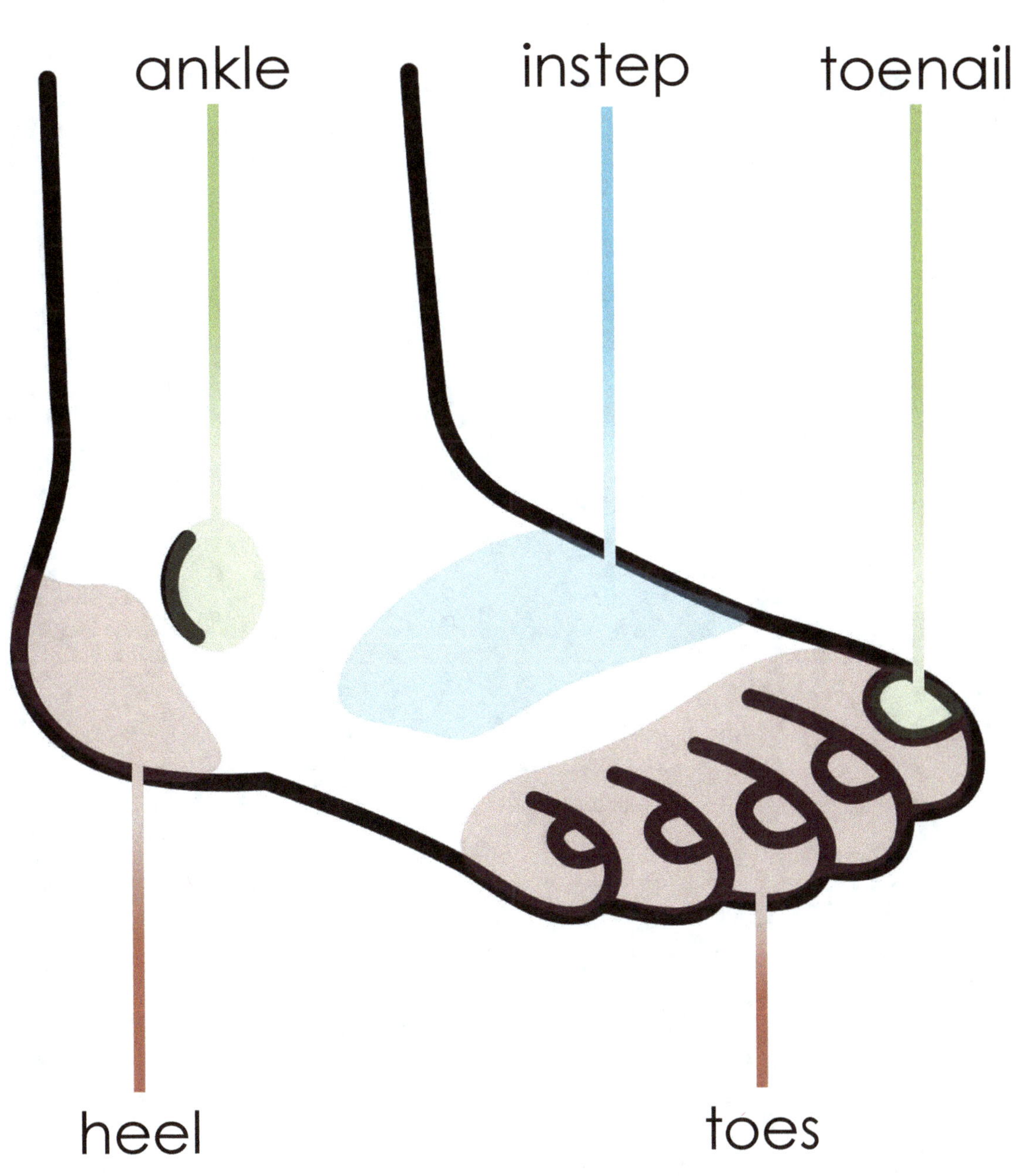

Appendix

Days of the Week

Weekdays

Monday
Tuesday
Wednesday
Thursday
Friday

Weekend

Saturday
Sunday

Months of the Year

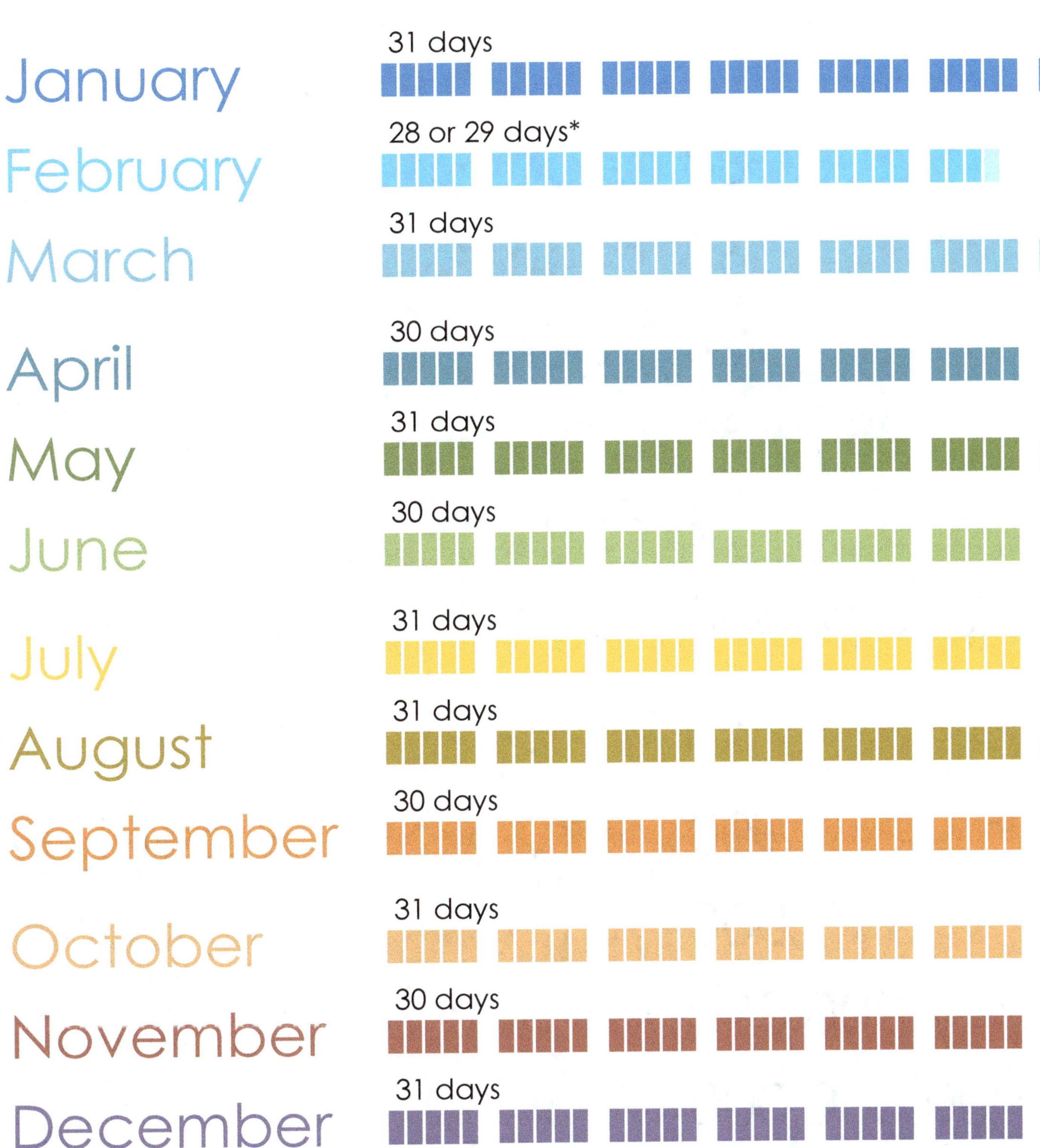

*February has 28 days,
unless the number of the year is divisible by 4, in which case February has 29 days,
unless the number of the year is divisible by 100, in which case February has 28 days,
unless the number of the year is divisible by 400, in which case February has 29 days.

Time Conversions

			1	second
60	seconds	=	1	minute
60	minutes	=	1	hour
24	hours	=	1	day
28 to 31	days	=	1	month
12	months	=	1	year
365 or 366	days*	=	1	year
10	years	=	1	decade
100	years	=	1	century
1,000	years	=	1	millenium
1,000,000	years	=	1	epoch
1,000,000,000	years	=	1	eon

*A year has 365 days,
unless the number of the year is divisible by 4, in which case a year has 366 days,
unless the number of the year is divisible by 100, in which case a year has 365 days,
unless the number of the year is divisible by 400, in which case a year has 366 days.

Solar System

Earth

Western Hemisphere

Earth

Eastern Hemisphere

Greek Alphabet

Letter	Name	Sound
Αα	**alpha**	a
Ββ	**beta**	b
Γγ	**gamma**	y
Δδ	**delta**	th as in *this*
Εε	**epsilon**	short e
Ζζ	**zeta**	z
Ηη	**eta**	long e
Θθ	**theta**	th as in tee*th*
Ιι	**iota**	short i
Κκ	**kappa**	k
Λλ	**lambda**	l
Μμ	**mu**	m
Νν	**nu**	n
Ξξ	**xi**	ks
Οο	**omicron**	long o
Ππ	**pi**	p
Ρρ	**rho**	rolling r
Σς	**sigma**	s
Ττ	**tau**	t
Υυ	**upsilon**	long u
Φφ	**phi**	f
Χχ	**chi**	hard h
Ψψ	**psi**	ps
Ωω	**omega**	short o

Cyrillic Alphabet

(Russian)

Аа	Бб	Вв	Гг	Дд	Ее
a short a	**be** b	**ve** v	**ghe** g	**de** d	**ie** short e

Жж	Зз	Ии	Кк	Лл
zhe z as in azure	**ze** z	**i** long e	**ka** k	**el** l

Мм	Нн	Оо	Пп	Рр
em m	**en** n	**o** short o	**pe** p	**er** r

Сс	Тт	Уу	Фф	Хх
es s	**te** t	**u** u as in tune	**ef** f	**ha** hard h

Цц	Чч	Шш	Щщ	Ъъ
tse ts	**che** ch	**sha** hard sh	**shcha** soft sh	hard sign

Ыы	Ьь	Ээ	Юю	Яя
yeru short i	soft sign	**e** short e	**yu** u as in use	**ya** y or ya

Hebrew Alphabet

alef
a

bet
b

gimel
g

dalet
d

he
h

vav
v

zayin
z

het
sharp h

tet
t

yod
y

kaf
k

lamed
l

mem
m

nun
n

samekh
s

ayin
hard stop

pe
p

tsadi
ts

qof
q

resh
r

shin
sh

tav
t

Arabic Alphabet

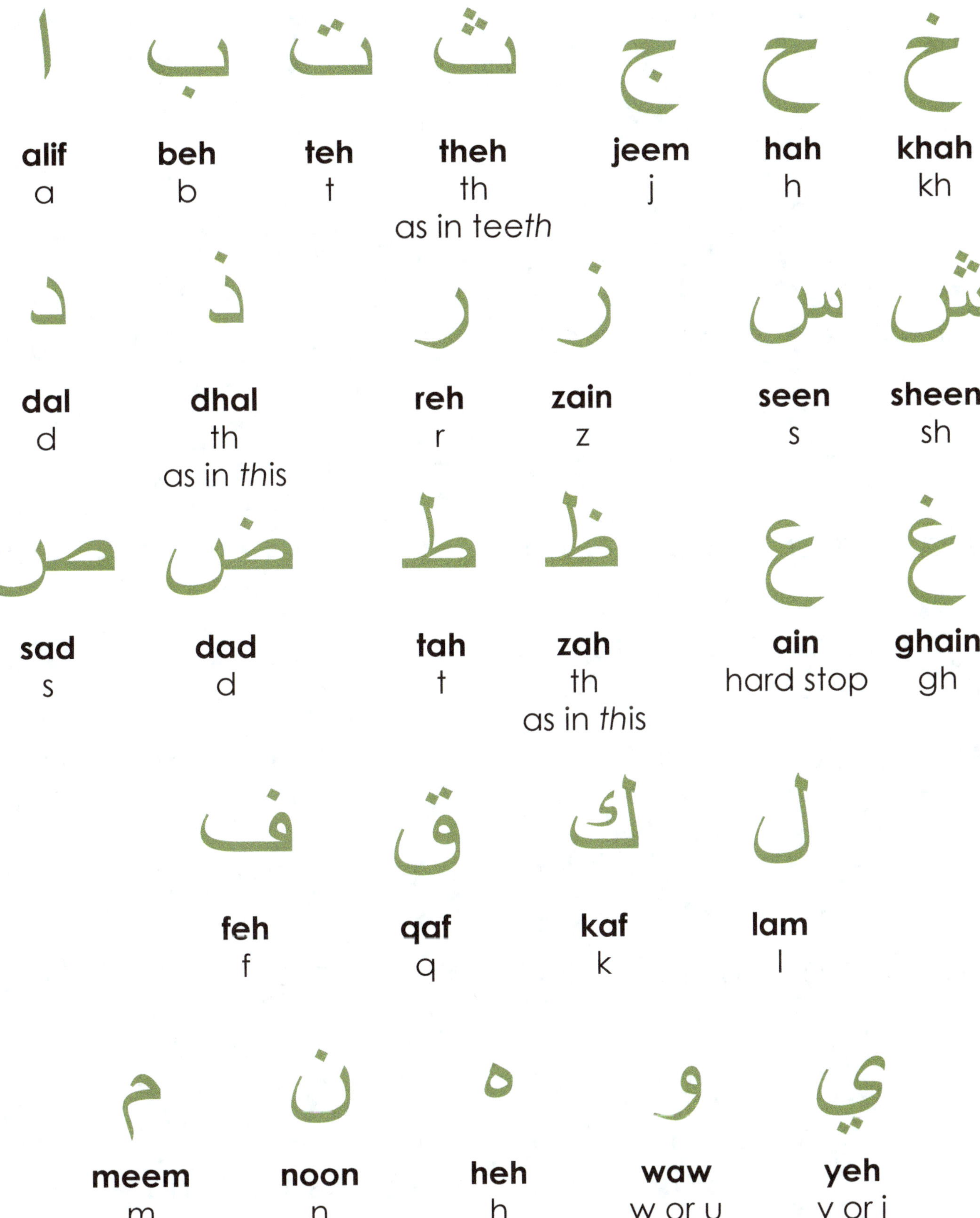

Hindi Alphabet

अ	आ	इ	ई	उ	ऊ	ऋ	ए
a	aa	i	ee	u	oo	ri	e
ऐ	ओ	औ	अं	अः	क	ख	ग
ai	o	au	an	ah	ka	kha	ga
घ	ङ	च	छ	ज	झ	ञ	ट
gha	nga	ca	cha	ja	jha	nya	tta
ठ	ड	ढ	ण	त	थ	द	ध
ttha	da	dha	nna	ta	tha	da	dha
न	प	फ	ब	भ	म	य	र
na	pa	pha	ba	bha	ma	ya	ra
ल	व	श	ष	स	ह		
la	va	sha	ssa	sa	ha		

Myanmar Alphabet

က ka	ခ kha	ဂ ga	ဃ gha	င nga
စ ca	ဆ cha	ဇ ja	ဈ jha	ည nnya
ဋ tta	ဌ ttha	ဍ dda	ဎ ddha	ဏ nna
တ ta	ထ tha	ဒ da	ဓ dha	န na
ပ pa	ဖ pha	ဗ ba	ဘ bha	မ ma
ယ ya	ရ ra	လ la	ဝ wa	သ sa
	ဟ ha	ဠ lla	အ a	

ကာ ka
ကိ ki
ကီ kii
ကု ku
ကူ kuu
ကေ ke
ကဲ kai

Korean Alphabet

	ㄱ g	ㄴ n	ㄷ d	ㄹ r	ㅁ m	ㅂ b	ㅅ s	ㅇ silent	ㅈ j	ㅊ ch	ㅋ k	ㅌ t	ㅍ p	ㅎ h
ㅏ a	가 ga	나 na	다 da	라 ra	마 ma	바 ba	사 sa	아 a	자 ja	차 cha	카 ka	타 ta	파 pa	하 ha
ㅑ ya	갸 gya	냐 nya	댜 dya	랴 rya	먀 mya	뱌 bya	샤 sya	야 ya	쟈 jya	챠 chya	캬 kya	탸 tya	퍄 pya	햐 hya
ㅓ eo	거 geo	너 neo	더 deo	러 reo	머 meo	버 beo	서 seo	어 eo	저 jeo	처 cheo	커 keo	터 teo	퍼 peo	허 heo
ㅕ yeo	겨 gyeo	녀 nyeo	뎌 dyeo	려 ryeo	며 myeo	벼 byeo	셔 syeo	여 yeo	져 jyeo	쳐 chyeo	켜 kyeo	텨 tyeo	펴 pyeo	혀 hyeo
ㅗ o	고 go	노 no	도 do	로 ro	모 mo	보 bo	소 so	오 o	조 jo	초 cho	코 ko	토 to	포 po	호 ho
ㅛ yo	교 gyo	뇨 nyo	됴 dyo	료 ryo	묘 myo	뵤 byo	쇼 syo	요 yo	죠 jyo	쵸 chyo	쿄 kyo	툐 tyo	표 pyo	효 hyo
ㅜ u	구 gu	누 nu	두 du	루 ru	무 mu	부 bu	수 su	우 u	주 ju	추 chu	쿠 ku	투 tu	푸 pu	후 hu
ㅠ yu	규 gyu	뉴 nyu	듀 dyu	류 ryu	뮤 myu	뷰 byu	슈 syu	유 yu	쥬 jyu	츄 chyu	큐 kyu	튜 tyu	퓨 pyu	휴 hyu
ㅡ eu	그 geu	느 neu	드 deu	르 reu	므 meu	브 beu	스 seu	으 eu	즈 jeu	츠 cheu	크 keu	트 teu	프 peu	흐 heu
ㅣ i	기 gi	니 ni	디 di	리 ri	미 mi	비 bi	시 si	이 i	지 ji	치 chi	키 ki	티 ti	피 pi	히 hi
ㅐ ae	개 gae	내 nae	대 dae	래 rae	매 mae	배 bae	새 sae	애 ae	재 jae	채 chae	캐 kae	태 tae	패 pae	해 hae

Runic Alphabet

(Anglo Saxon)

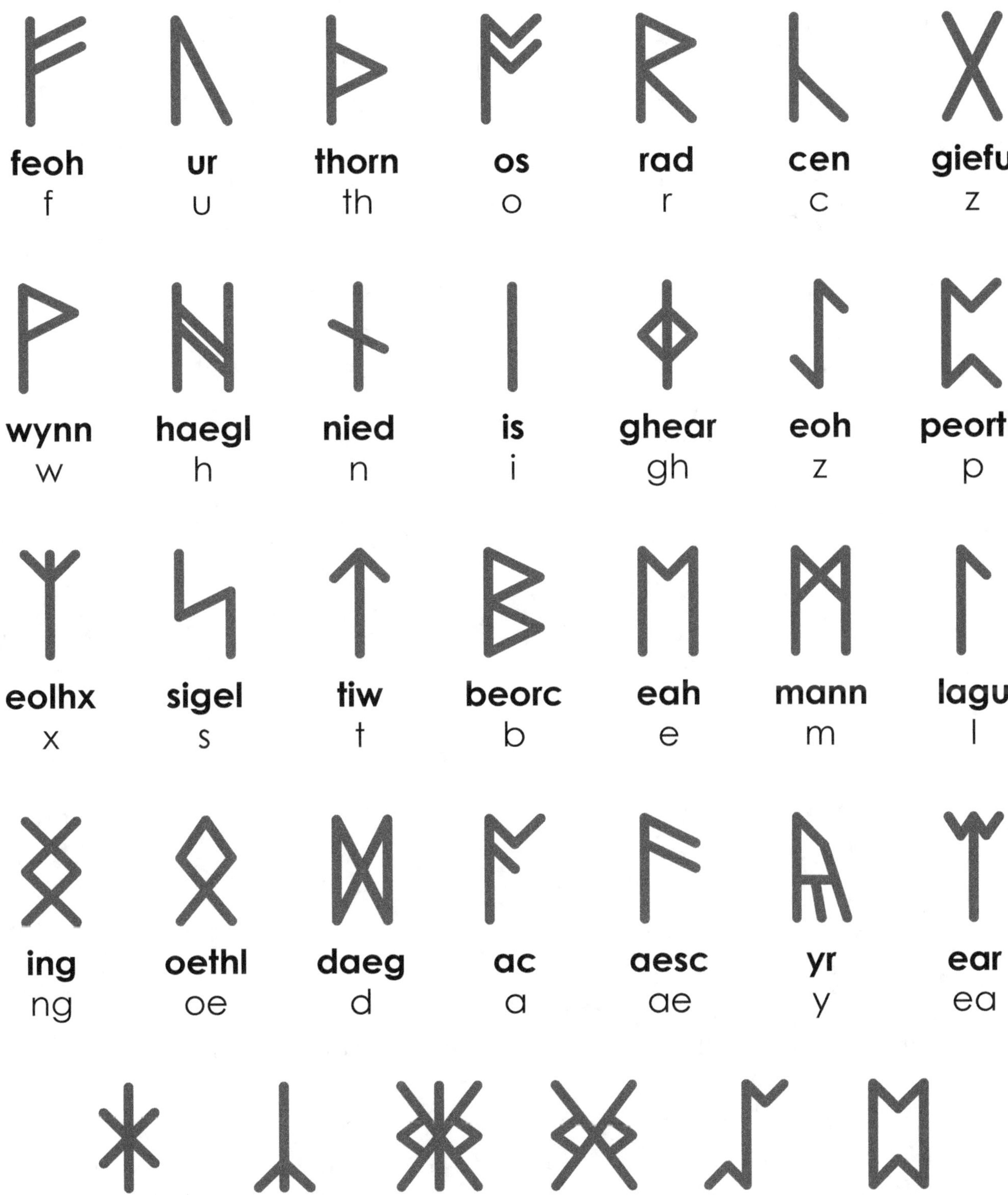

Braille Alphabet

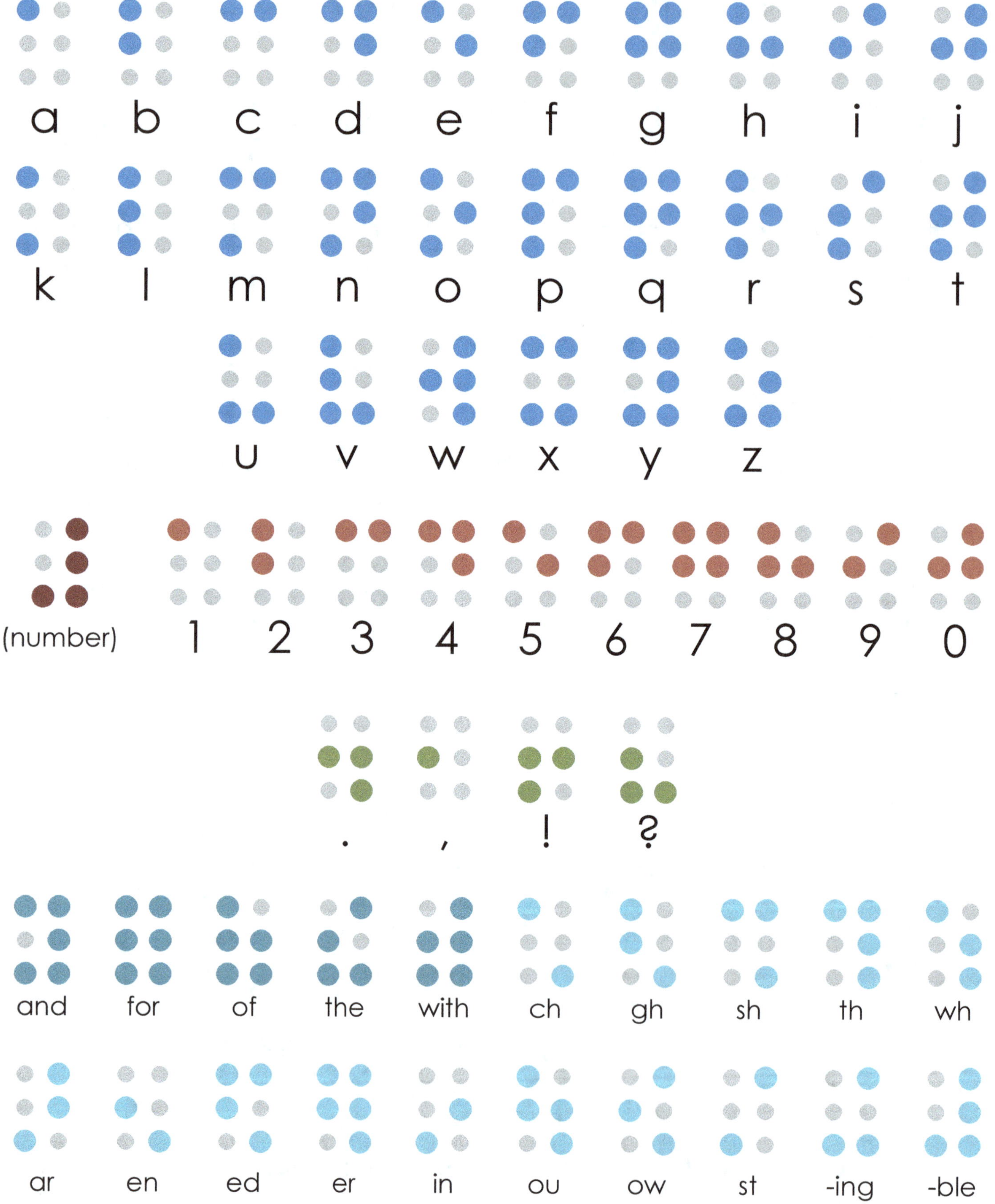

ASL Alphabet

(American Sign Language)

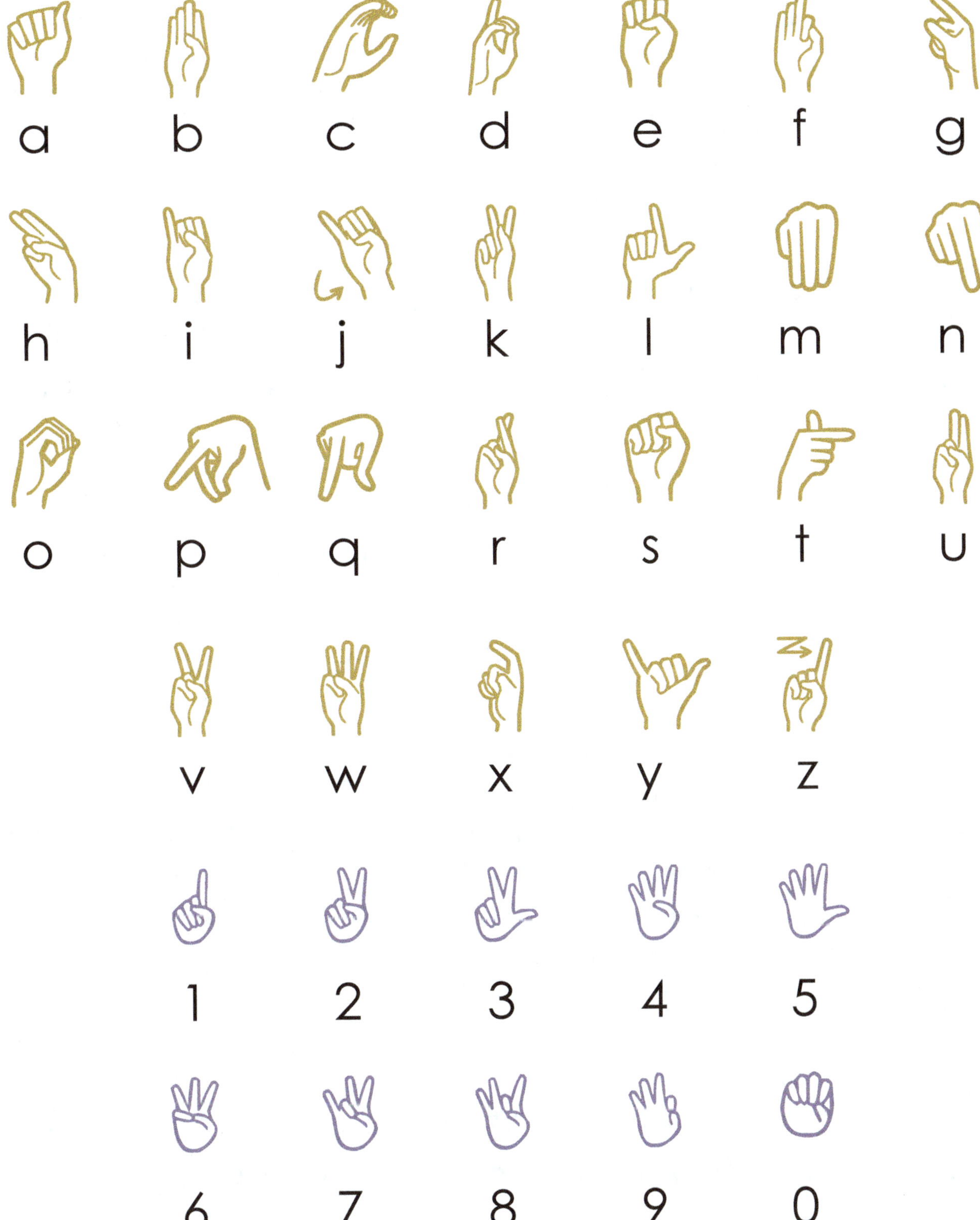

Egyptian Hieroglyphics

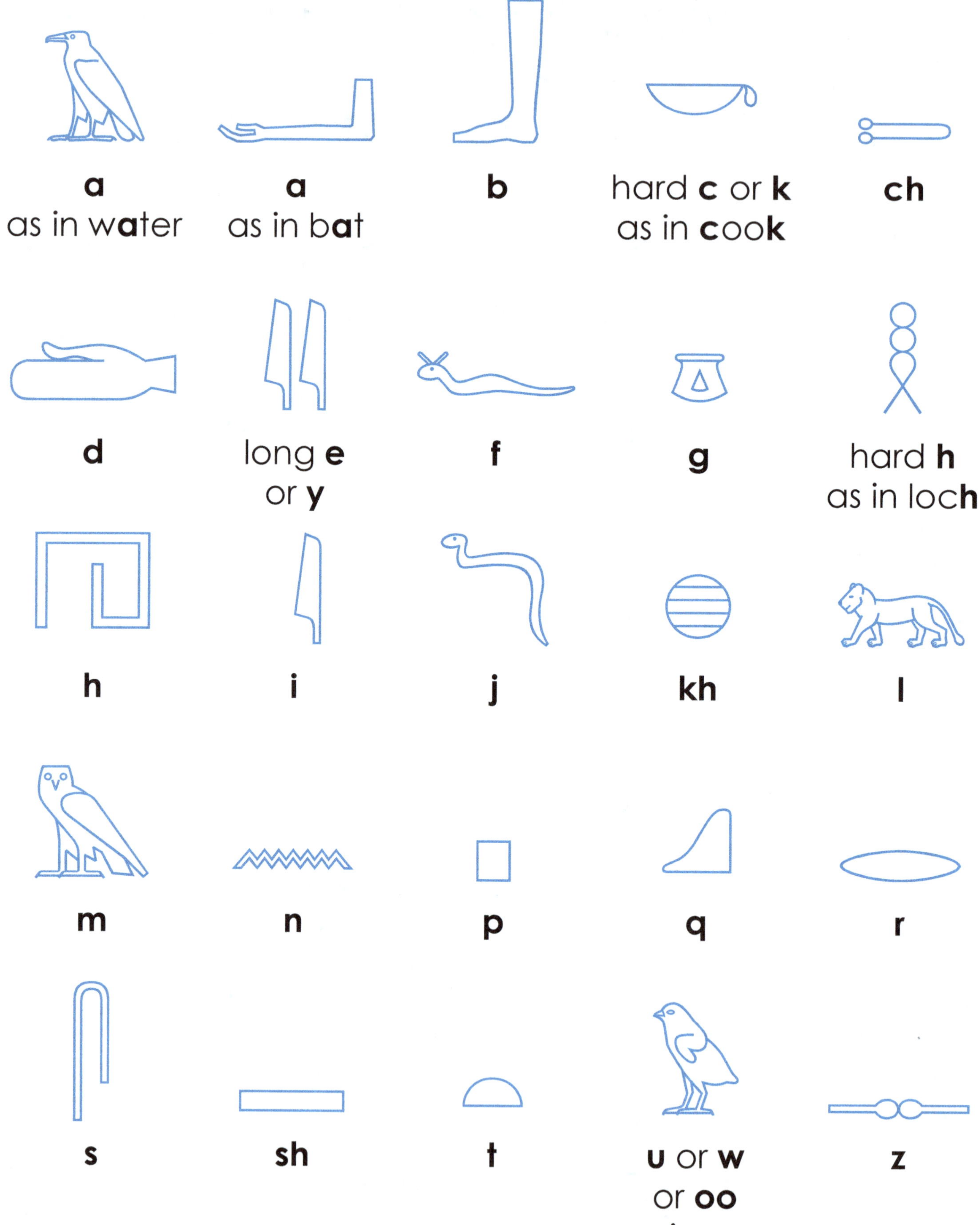

Morse Code

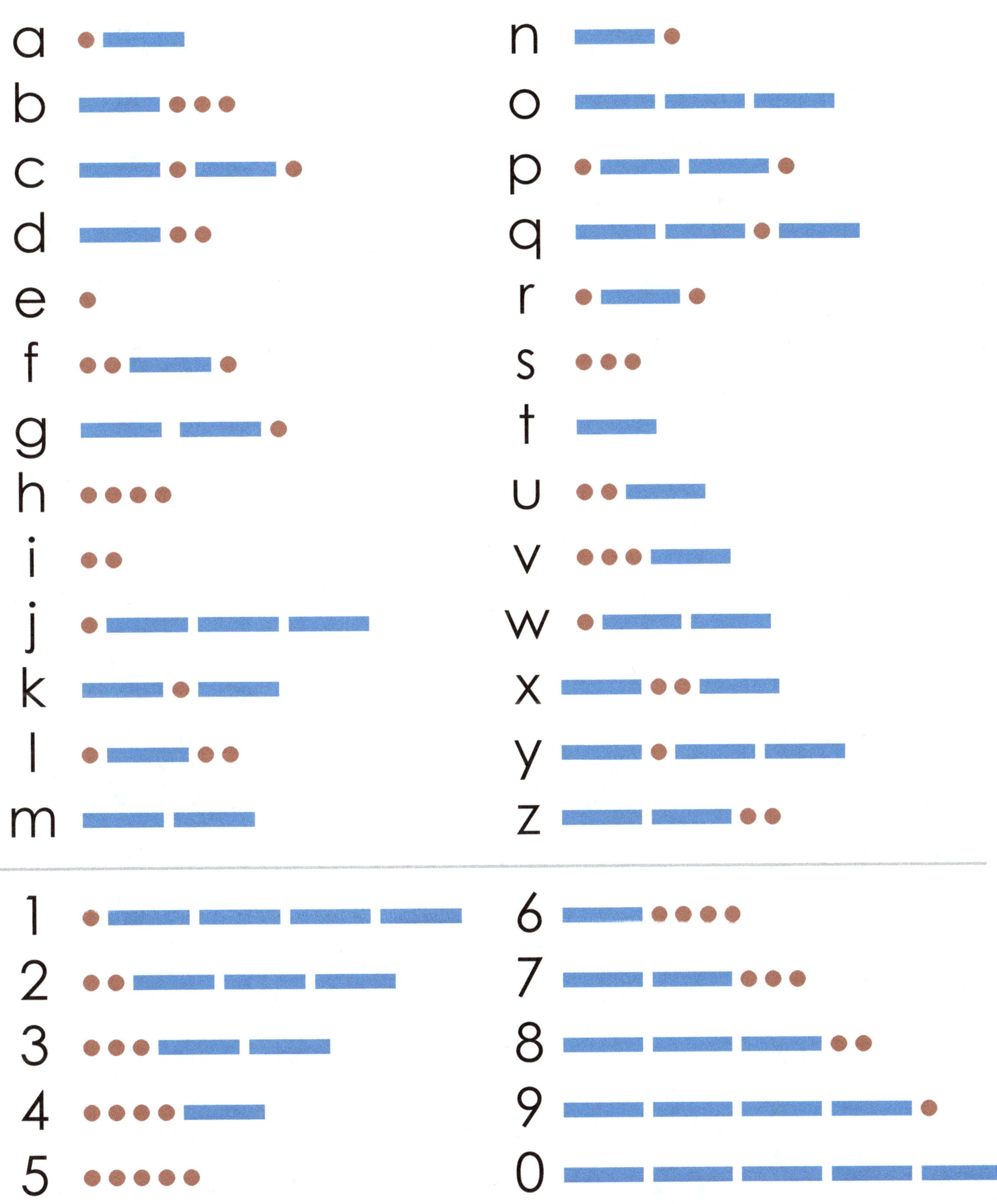

Roman Numerals

I = 1
II = 2
III = 3
IV = 4
V = 5
VI = 6
VII = 7
VIII = 8
IX = 9
X = 10
XI = 11
XII = 12
XIII = 13
XIV = 14
XV = 15
XVI = 16
XVII = 17
XVIII = 18
XIX = 19

XX = 20
XXI = 21
XXII = 22
XXIII = 23
XXIV = 24
XXV = 25
XXVI = 26
XXVII = 27
XXVIII = 28
XXIX = 29
XXX = 30
XL = 40
L = 50
LX = 60
LXX = 70
LXXX = 80
XC = 90
C = 100
CI = 101

CL = 150
CC = 200
CCC = 300
CD = 400
D = 500
DC = 600
DCC = 700
DCCC = 800
CM = 900
M = 1000
MI = 1001
MV = 1005
MX = 1010
ML = 1050
MC = 1100
MD = 1500
MCM = 1900
MM = 2000
MMM = 3000

Mayan Numerals

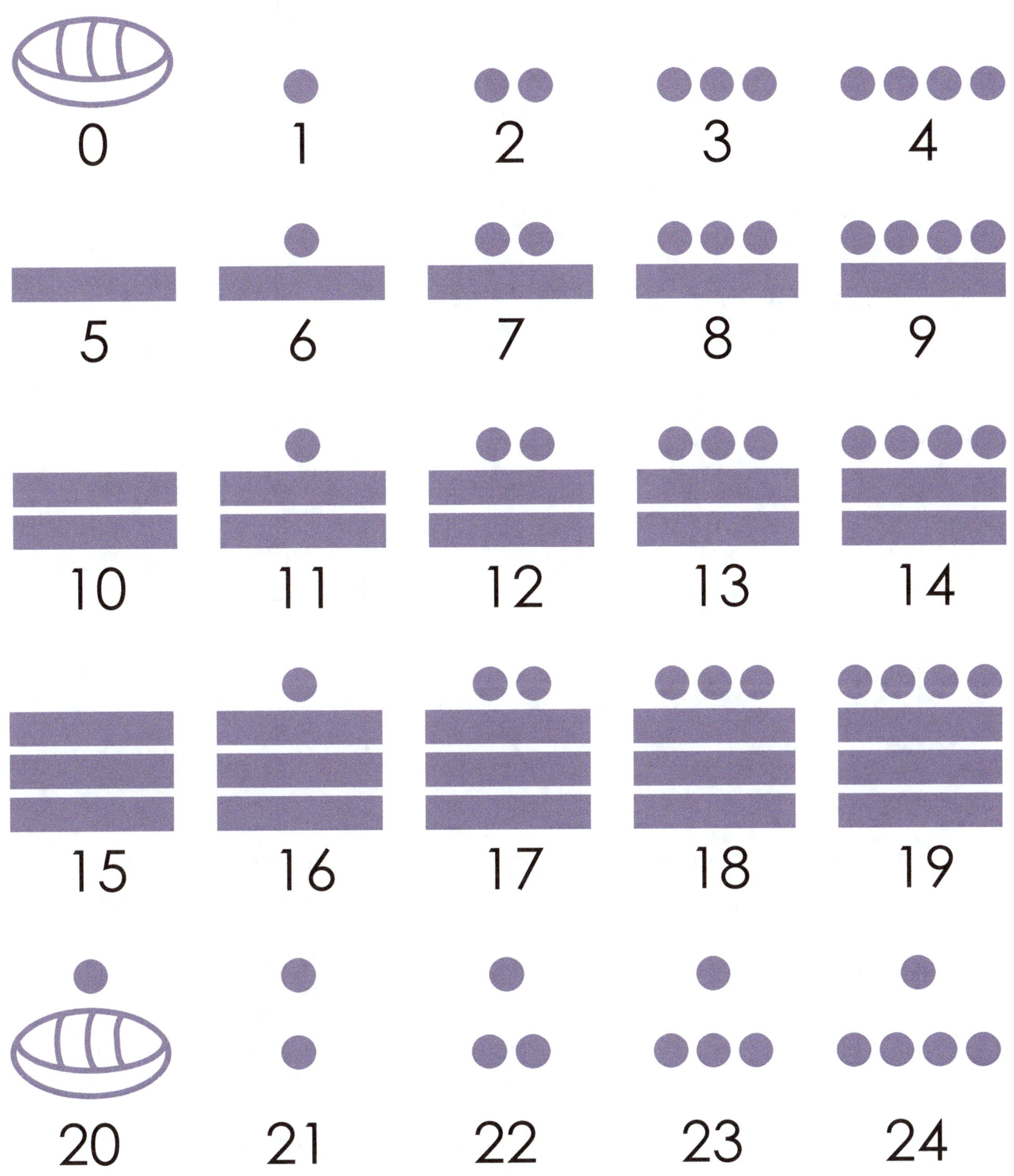

Music Symbols

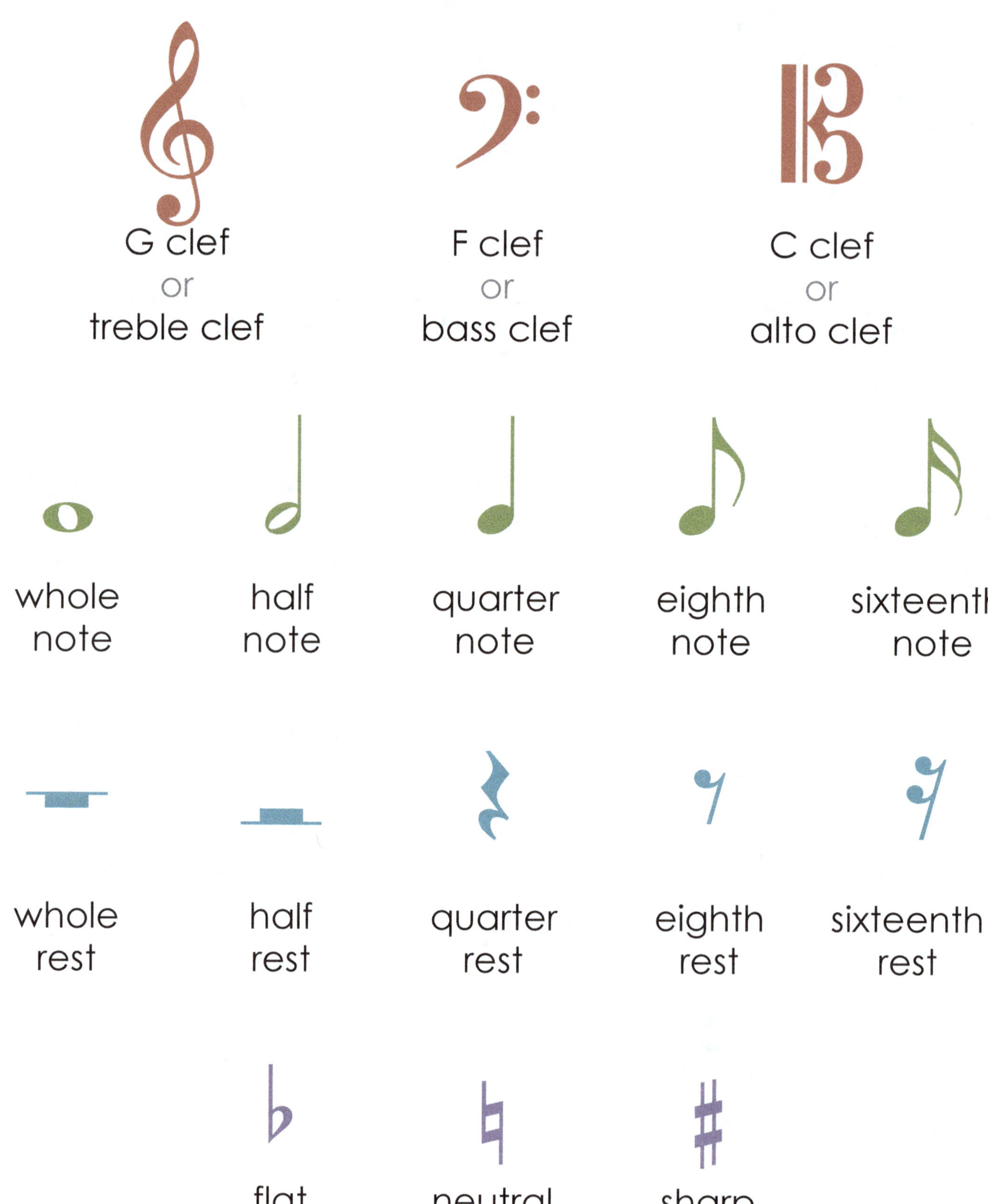

Acknowledgements

This book was created completely in Microsoft Visio. The pie charts in the Numbers section were created with Microsoft Excel.

The brain vector graphic used on the cover and inside this book is from the svgrepo.com web site, specifically the "Brain SVG Vector 72" graphic. https://www.svgrepo.com/svg/156615/brain.

Artwork for the Body Parts section was purchased from Etsy.com. The seller is ClipArtisan, and the artwork is called "Body Parts Clipart Senses Anatomy Clip Art Human Body PNG SVG Instant Download 0029". https://www.etsy.com/listing/1171698075/body-parts-clipart-senses-anatomy-clip.

Images of the sun, moon, and planets in the Appendix section are from Microsoft Office's online Creative Commons image gallery.

The main font used throughout this book is Century Gothic, which I chose for its ball-and-stick simplicity. In the Letters section, I used a variety of other fonts. From top to bottom on the left side of each page, I used Rockwell, Arial Rounded Medium, Segoe Print, and Old English Text. From top to bottom on the right side of each page, I used Times New Roman, OpenDyslexic, Learning Curve, and Edwardian Script. All of these come standard with Microsoft Office, with the exception of OpenDyslexic and Cedarville Cursive.

OpenDyslexic is designed to be more easily read by people with some forms of dyslexia. You'll note how each of the letters is thicker at the bottom. This font can be found at https://opendyslexic.org.

Learning Curve can be found on FontSpace: https://www.fontspace.com/learning-curve-bv-font-f963. I chose to include this font because I thought young minds still might want to see what cursive letters look like, even though cursive handwriting is considered by many to be a dying art. It's still not exactly the same cursive that I grew up learning, but it was the closest thing I could find in font form.

The hieroglyphics phonetic translations shown herein came from egyptabout.com: https://www.egyptabout.com/p/hieroglyphics.html. The font used is Noto Sans Egyptian Hieroglyphics from Google Fonts: https://fonts.google.com/noto/specimen/Noto+Sans+Egyptian+Hieroglyphs, used in conjunction with Wikipedia: https://en.wikipedia.org/wiki/List_of_Egyptian_hieroglyphs.

The American Sign Language letters – that is, the images of the hands making the ASL letters – comes from https://fontmeme.com/fonts/american-sign-language-font/#google_vignette.

Regarding the colors used in the Colors section, I recognize that some of these colors and their names may not match everyone's perceptions. This was brought to my attention by my mother, Emily James, who's been an artist for over 50 years, and whose opinion therefore I trust in many matters (as my mother), but in color-related matters specifically (as an artist).

Despite that, the colors I used here is my best attempt to align with what appears to be an emerging standard. Specifically, I used Microsoft's Bing search engine to determine the hexadecimal code for each color. Where Bing identified three or more sources that agreed on the hexadecimal code for a color, I used that. Where no clear standard existed, I used the hexadecimal codes suggested by htmlcolorcodes.com. For the colors not represented on htmlcolorcodes.com, I used the code suggested by color-name.com.

On that note, you should visit my mother's art web site, www.emilyjamesart.com. She's really good.

www.ingramcontent.com/pod-product-compliance
Lightning Source LLC
Chambersburg PA
CBHW082019150726
48196CB00073B/549